How to T

A Beginner's Guide to investing and making profit with Options Trading

Warren Ray Benjamin

Table Of Contents

How to Trade Options:

Day Trading Strategies

Warren Ray Benjamin

Table Of Contents

How to Trade Options:

Swing Trading

Warren Ray Benjamin

Table Of Contents

Introduction

Welcome to How to Trade Options: A Beginner's Guide. In this book, we'll introduce you to the exciting and challenging world of options. While options involve higher risk-taking than normal stock market investing, they are also more interesting and exciting, with a huge potential upside. Some of the topics we'll be discussing in this book include:

- Learning what options are and the entire industry lingo.
- Find out the top reasons to trade options.
- Answer the question: Is trading options really for you?
- Learn to avoid common mistakes made by beginners.
- Find out the best strategies for beginners in the Markets.

And much more!

By the time you finish this book, you should understand how options work, how and where to trade them, and be able to converse like an expert. You'll also know the strategies used by the pros to trade options and profit handsomely and how to apply them yourself.

Options' trading is not for everyone. Before you jump in, you should study options carefully, so you know what you're getting into. While options can help you gain profits quickly as compared to normal stock trading which is a long-term endeavor, there is heightened risk.

- Understand your risk profile: If you are not a risk taker and see bonds and mutual funds as places where you want to put your money, options might be too risky for you. However, you should learn about them first. There are options...when it comes to options that can help reduce risk, so there may be a place for you in the space. It is best to learn it firsthand to get a better idea of what your profile is and how you prefer to trade.

- Understand your financial situation: Before jumping into any new investment program, make sure you have a clear picture of where you stand financially. You should know where you are at for income, credit card debts, taxes, other loans, and obligations. Have a clear idea of how much capital you can really afford to lose.

- Be an analyst, not a careless risk taker: Options require a deeper understanding of the markets than regular stock trading does. The excitement that arises from the possibility of fast and large profits can overwhelm some people, leading to excessive risk-taking. Be aware of this and put the time in to do analysis rather than looking only for a fast buck.

- Don't invest money you aren't willing to lose. Before engaging in options trading, make sure you're not gambling with money you need for essentials.

Please note that while we're bullish on options trading, all trading and investment activity carries with it some risk. If done correctly, a trader can earn substantial profits from their activities; however, some traders will be at risk of losing substantial amounts of money. No guarantees can be made, and the topics discussed in this book are presented for informational and educational purposes only and are not to be taken as actual financial advice. The best teacher yet experiences and once you know the basics, it is time to get your feet wet and apply what you have learned!

Chapter 1: Options Contracts: The Basics

In this chapter, we will introduce the concept of options contracts and how they are used in the stock market. In our introductory discussion, we will be focusing on the most basic way to get involved in options, which involves buying options contracts based on bets you make on whether future stock prices will rise or fall. Later we will see that you can also write or sell options contracts and that the contracts themselves are traded on the markets.

What is an Options Contract?

An options contract sounds fancy but it's a pretty simple concept.

- It's a contract. That means it's a legal agreement between a buyer and a seller.

- It gives the purchaser of the contract the opportunity to purchase or dispose of an asset with a fixed amount.
- The purchase is optional – so the buyer of the contract does not have to buy or sell the asset.
- The contract has an expiration date, so the purchaser – if they choose to exercise their right – must make the trade on or before the expiration date.
- The purchaser of the contract pays a non-refundable fee for the contract.

While the focus of this book is on options contracts related to the stock market, there are options contracts that take place in all aspects of daily life including real estate and speculation. A simple example illustrates the concept of an options contract.

Suppose you are itching to buy a BMW and you've decided the model you want must be silver. You drop by a local dealer and it turns out they don't have a silver model in stock. The dealer claims he can get you one by the end of the month. You say you'll take the car if the dealer can get it by the last day of the month and he'll sell it to you for $67,500. He agrees and requires you to put a $3,000 deposit on the car.

If the last day of the month arrives and the dealer hasn't produced the car, then you're freed from the contract and get your money back. In the event he does produce the car at any date before the end of the month, you have the option to buy it or not. If you really wanted the car you can buy it, but of course, you can't be forced to buy the car, and maybe you've changed your mind in the interim.

The right is there but not the obligation to purchase, in short, no pressure if you decided not to push through with the purchase of the car. If you decide to let the opportunity pass, however, since the dealer met his end of the bargain and produced the car, you lose the $3,000 deposit.

In this case, the dealer, who plays the role of the writer of the contract, *has the obligation to follow through with the sale* based upon the agreed upon price.

Suppose that when the car arrives at the dealership, BMW announces it will no longer make silver cars. As a result, prices of new silver BMWs that were the last ones to roll off the assembly line, skyrocket. Other dealers are selling their silver BMWs for $100,000. However, since this dealer entered into an options contract with you, he must sell the car to you for the pre-agreed price of $67,500. You decide to get the car and drive away smiling, knowing that you saved $32,500 and that you could sell it at a profit if you wanted to.

The situation here is capturing the essence of options contracts, even if you've never thought of haggling with a car dealer in those terms.

An option is in a sense a kind of bet. In the example of the car, the bet is that the dealer can produce the exact car you want within the specified time period and at the agreed upon price. The dealer is betting too. His bet is that the pre-agreed to price is a good one for him. Of course, if BMW stops making silver cars, then he's made the wrong bet.

It can work the other way too. Let's say that instead of BMW deciding not to make silver cars anymore when your car is being driven onto the lot, another car crashes into it. Now your silver BMW has a small dent on the rear bumper with some scratches. As a result, the car has immediately declined in value. But if you want the car, since you've agreed to the options contract, you must pay $67,500, even though with the dent it's only really worth $55,000. You can walk away and lose your $3,000 or pay what is now a premium price on a damaged car.

Another example that is commonly used to explain options contracts is the purchase of a home to be built by a developer under the agreement that certain conditions are met. The buyer will be required to put a non-refundable down payment or deposit on the home. Let's say that the developer agrees to build them the home for $300,000 provided that a new school is built within 5 miles of the development within one year. So, the contract expires within a year. At any time during the year, the buyer has the option to go forward with the construction of the home for $300,000 if the school is built. The developer has agreed to the price no matter what. So if the housing market in general and the construction of the school, in particular, drive up demand for housing in the area, and the developer is selling new homes that are now priced at $500,000, he has to sell this home for $300,000 because that was the price agreed to when the contract was signed. The home buyer got what they wanted, being within 5 miles of the new school with the home price fixed at $300,000. The developer was assured of the sale but missed out on the unknown, which was the skyrocketing price that occurred as a result of increased demand. On the other hand, if the school isn't built and the buyers don't exercise their option to buy the house before the contract expires at one year, the developer can pocket the $20,000 cash.

What is an options contract on the stock market?

An options contract on the stock market is somewhat analogous to the fictitious situation we just described with the car. In the case of the car, we saw that unforeseen events can make the bet made by the buyer and the car dealer profitable or not. The same thing happens in the stock market. Of course in the case of the car, the buyer is simply hoping to get the car they want at what they perceive to be a bargain price, although if BMW really stopped making silver cars, they might sell it to a third party and then get a white one from the dealer. However, in most cases, the buyer wants the car. That isn't the case when it comes to options with stocks.

On the stock market, we are betting on the future price itself, and the shares of stock will be bought or sold at a profit if things work out. The key point is the buyer of the options contract is not hoping to acquire the

11

shares and hold them for a long time period like a traditional investor. Instead, you're hoping to make a bet on the price of the stock, secure that price, and then be able to trade the shares on that price no matter what happens on the actual markets. We will illustrate this with an example.

CALL Options

A call is a type of option contract that provides the option to purchase an asset at the agreed upon amount at the designated time or deadline. The reason you would do this is if you felt that the price of a given stock would increase in price over the specified time period. Let's illustrate with an example.

Suppose that Acme Communications makes cutting edge smartphones. The rumors are that they will announce a new smartphone in the next three weeks that is going to take the market by storm, with customers lined out the door to make preorders.

The current price that Acme Communications is trading at is $44.25 a share. The current pricing of an asset is termed as the *spot price*. Put another way, the spot price is the actual amount that you would be paying for the shares as you would buy it from the stock market right now.

Nobody really knows if the stock price will go up when the announcement is made, or if the announcement will even be made. But you've done your research and are reasonably confident these events will take place. You also have to estimate how much the shares will go up and based on your research you think it's going to shoot up to $65 a share by the end of the month.

You enter into an options contract for 100 shares at $1 per share. You pay this fee to the brokerage that is writing the options contract. In total, for 100 shares you pay $100.

The price that is paid for an options contract is $100. This price is called the *premium*.

You don't get the premium back. It's a fee that you pay no matter what. If you make a profit, then it's all good. But if your bet is wrong, then you'll lose the premium. For the buyer of an options contract, the premium is their risk.

You'll want to set a price that you think is going to be lower than the level to which the price per share will rise. The price that you agree to is called the *strike price.* For this contract, you set your strike price at $50.

Remember, exercising your right to buy the shares is optional. You'll only buy the shares if the price goes high enough that you'll make a profit on the trade. If the shares never go above $50, say they reach $48, you are not obligated to buy them. And why would you? As part of the contract deal, you'd be required to buy them at $50.

We'll say that the contract is entered on the 1st of August, and the deadline is the third Friday in August.

If the price goes higher than your strike price during that time, you can exercise your option.

Let's say that as the deadline approaches, things go basically as you planned. Acme Communications announces its new phone, and the stock starts climbing. The stock price on the actual market (the spot price) goes up to $60.

Now the seller is required to sell you the shares at $50 a share. You buy the shares, and then you can immediately dispose of these at a quality or optimal amount, or $60 a share. You make a profit of $10 a share, not taking into account any commissions or fees.

The Call Seller

The call seller who enters into the options contract with the buyer is obligated to sell the shares to the buyer of the options contract at the strike price. If the contract sets the strike price at $50 a share for 100 shares, the seller must sell the stock at that price even if the market price goes up to any higher price, such as $70 a share. The call seller keeps the premium. So, if the buyer doesn't exercise their option, the call seller still gets the money from the premium.

Derivative Contracts

You probably heard about derivatives or derivative contracts during the 2008 financial crisis. While they can be designed in complex ways, the concept of a derivative contract is pretty simple. What this means is that the contract is based on some underlying asset. For an options contract, the asset is the stock that you agree to buy or sell. The contracts themselves can and are bought and sold. That is why you may have heard about people trading in derivatives. The stock that is the subject of an options contract is called the *underlying*.

So, if you buy an options contract using the Apple stock price as a basis, the term "underlying" would be applicable to the stock from Apple.

Profits from the Call

Keep in mind the brokerage may have some additional fees. However, using our numbers remember that we paid a premium of $1 per share, and the strike price was $50. Computing for profit is one of the basics when it comes to trading. It is where profits are determined and forecasted for future options to buy or sell.

The profit per share was:

Profit = $60 − ($50 + $1) = $9 per share

The contract was for 100 shares, so the total profit would be $90.

What happens if the strike price isn't reached?

The strike price is the fundamental piece of information you need to keep in mind when trading options. If the strike price isn't reached, then the option will simply expire and be worthless. The difference between the current market price or spot price and the strike price is a measure of the profit per share that you will make.

For example, $100 is the price of the stock, and the strike price is $75, then the profit (disregarding fees) will be $25. If the strike price was $95, then the profit per share would only be $5. While the pay off from a strike price that is closer to the actual market price is smaller, it's more likely to pay off than a strike price that predicts a big move.

Why purchase a call option

The reason that you purchase an options contract is to reduce your risk. When you buy an options contract, the only money you're putting at risk is the premium. In the case of our hypothetical example, that is $100. If the stock doesn't surpass the strike price, you can simply walk away from the deal and only lose the $100.

You could, of course, buy the stocks outright and hope to profit. To buy 100 shares, you'll have to invest substantially more money:

100 x $44.25 = $4,425.

If the stock goes up value, then you'll make some money. However, suppose that your hunch about the markets was wrong. Maybe Acme Communications, rather than announcing a new phone that will be in high demand, instead reveals that their next phone will be delayed for a year.

If you decide to unload the stocks you bought for $4,425, you will only get $4,000, and you'll have lost $425.

On the other hand, you can see how you reduced your risk by purchasing a call option. In that case, you won't exercise your right to buy the stock and only lose the premium. Your total loss would be $100.

The Flexibility of Options
In normal stock trading, you're betting on one direction, that the value of the stock will go up with

time. And you're battling the opposite, hoping to avoid losses if the stock declines.

Options open the door to making a profit when stocks decline in value. Of course, it depends on being able to make the right call, but if you bet on a stock losing value and you're right, you can make substantial profits. Timing and the size of your trade will be important too, and you'll have to stay focused on the strike price and the current market price of the underlying.

Put Options

A call option is the option to buy a stock if it reaches the strike price. Now let's look at the opposite situation. A *put* is an option contract where you get the right but not the obligation to *sell* a stock before the contract expires. Returning to our previous example, suppose that Acme Communications looks to be heading to bad times and the stock is trading at $44.25 a share. Your bet is that it's going to decrease to at least $35 a share, so you buy a put option with a strike price of $35 a share. If your bet that the stock will decline in value and you're correct, let's say it drops to $30 a share, then you can make a $5 per share profit on the sale. If the stock meets the strike price, the seller of the put is obligated to purchase the stock at that price. In other words, even though the stock has dropped in value to $30 a share on the market, they must buy the shares from you at $35 a share.

Let's suppose that instead it only drops to $38 a share. In this case, you don't have to sell and simply walk away from the deal having paid the premium. So once again, as was the case with a call option, the premium is really the only money that you risk as to the buyer.

The seller of a put option *must* buy the stock from you at the strike price if you exercise your option. If the strike price is $35 but for some reason, the stock crashes to $1, the seller of the put must buy the shares from you at $35.

Why Buy a Put Option?

The answer is simple – when you buy stocks the usual way, you don't make any money from the declining values of stocks. You lose money. With a put option, it gives you the possibility of betting on the stock losing value.

Summary: Buyers of Options

The buyer of an options contract:

- Must pay the premium. This is non-refundable, so the premium is the minimum amount of capital you invest and is the amount you risk.
- You are not obligated to buy or sell any stock even when the deadline arrives.
- You have purchased the right to buy or sell the stock.
- If you buy a call, then you have the option to purchase the expiry of the agreement. If you buy a put, you have the option to sell the stock when the expiry arrives. The option to sell only falls in

instances when there is a marked difference between the market price and your own strike price; with the market price being too low.

Summary: Sellers of Calls and Puts

Later we'll see that you may want to sell options and there are good reasons for doing so. Right now, we'll just summarize the general principles.

- The seller of an options contract will keep the premium no matter what. So, if the buyer doesn't exercise their option, you keep the premium as profit.

- If the buyer of a call option exercises their option to buy the stock, you must sell it to them at the strike price. So, if the strike price is $40 but the current market price is $65, you are missing out on a large profit per share. However, as we'll see later this can still be profitable.

- If the buyer exercises their right on a put contract, you must buy the stock from them at the deadline.

Number of Shares

The number of shares in one options contract is 100 shares. Typically, traders will trade multiple contracts. To you'll get the profit per share and then calculate total profit as (profit per share * 100 shares * # of contracts).

Now let's get familiar with the industry jargon so you can have a better understanding of what is going on when you start trading.

Chapter 2: Options Trading Jargon

Every industry has its own specialized lingo, and options trading is no exception. Let's give a quick overview that will help you understand what is being discussed when reading about options and help you navigate the markets effectively.

Ask

The price that a seller is asking for security or put another way the smallest price a seller is willing to accept to sell it.

Assignment

When the buyer of an options contract exercises their option, a notice is sent to the seller. The seller is then obligated to dispose of (in the case of a call) or purchase (in the case of a put) stocks at the strike price.

At the Money

This means that the current market price is equal to the strike price.

Bid Price

This term refers to the optimum amount that a dealer is willing to shell out for the security.

Break Even Point

When neither a profit nor loss has been realized.

Call

Summarizing what was introduced in the last chapter, the buyer of a call option has the right to buy 100 shares of a stock at the strike price at any time before the options contract expires. This is an option, so the buyer does not have to buy the shares. The seller of a call contract must buy the shares under any circumstances up to the expiration of the contract if the buyer exercises their right before the contract expires.

Commission

A fee charged by a brokerage firm to execute an option order on an exchange.

Delta

If the underlying stock changes by a point in value, the delta is the change in the value of the option.

Early Exercise

If an options contract is exercised before the expiration date, it is said to be early.

Exercise

The buyer of the option exercises their right to buy stock for a call or sell the stock for a put.

Expiration Date

Options contracts expire on the third Friday of every month. When you see an option quote such as:

JUN 70

That means that the option expires on the third Friday in June, with a strike price of $70.

In the Money (Call)

This refers to the occurrence of when the current market price exceeds the strike price. This is the gross profit per share (not including premium and other fees).

In the Money (Put)

For a put contract, it is in-the-money when the current stock price is less than the strike price.

Index Options

An index option doesn't have individual stocks as the underlying. Instead the underlying is an index like the NASDAQ. An index option can't be exercised until the expiry date.

Intrinsic Value

An apt example would be – if the current price is at $10, then the market price is at $20, the intrinsic value would be $10. If the current price were $25, the intrinsic value would be $15.

LEAP

A LEAP is a long-term equity anticipation security. Basically, these are long term options contracts. LEAP contracts can last as long as three years. LEAPS are generally more expensive than most options, because of the longtime value which gives them more time to be "in the money."

Legs

A leg is one part of a position when there are two or more options or positions in the underlying stock.

Long

Long means ownership when it is held in your account. You can belong on a stock or an option.

Margin Requirement

If you are selling options, you will be required to deposit some cash with the brokerage to cover your positions. In other words, it is cash in your account with the brokerage to buy or sell shares as required by your obligations in the options contract.

Option Chain

An option chain is something you'll look at when viewing available options online. It's basically a table for the options available for a given underlying stock. For given expiration date, the option chain will include all puts and calls, and strike prices that are available.

Out-of-the-Money

This is the amount that a stock price is below the strike price for a call, or above the strike price for a put. If your price $50 but the market is $40, you're "out of the money" $10. If your strike price for a put is $50, but the market price is $60, you're out of the money $10.

Premium

This is the price paid per share for an options contract. Since the contract has 100 shares, the price paid, or the total premium is 100 times the premium. The seller is able to keep the premium regardless of whether or not the buyer exercises their options.

Put

The buyer of a put option has the right to sell 100 shares at the strike price on or before the expiry date. The seller of a put option has an obligation to buy 100 shares if required by the buyer.

Roll a Long Position

Rolling a long position means to sell options and then acquire others with the same underlying stock but with different strike prices and expiration dates. We will talk a bit more about rolling options in the chapter on advanced trading strategies.

Roll a Short Position

Rolling a short position means buying to close an existing position and selling for the purposes of opening new positions with different strike prices and expiration dates "rolled out" in time.

Series

Options are grouped together in series on the markets. Options in the same series can be calls or puts, but they have the same expiration date and strike price.

Short

Selling a security that you don't actually own.

Strike Price

It is the amount per share of the agreed upon contract. If the option to buy or sell is exercised by the purchaser of an options contract, the shares must be bought or sold at the strike price. When you look at options online, the strike price is given at the end of the options symbol. For example, you might see:

00040000

The decimal point is found by moving three places from the right. So, this represents a strike price of $40. On the other hand

00005600

It would represent a strike price of $5.60.

Time Value

How long is left until an options contract expires? Generally, more time value will mean that an option is worth more when trading. The reason is that the more time until the option expires, the more chance there is for the underlying stock to beat the strike price. In the case of a call option that means going above the strike price, while in the case of a put option that means going below the strike price. What investors are looking for is enough time value for an option to be in the money.

Time Decay

Time decay is simply a measure of the decrease in the time value of an options contract.

Underlying

The underlying stock is the specific stock that the option contract is based on. This is the stock that is actually traded if the option is exercised.

Weekly

A weekly is a kind of option that expires within a week, rather than a monthly time frame. Since weekly's have a short time value, they are cheaper, but the risks involved are higher. Investors who like weekly's are hoping to capitalize on an option that tightly fits a given date coming up in the near future. Weeklies usually expire on Friday afternoons at market close. Weeklies help traders that are trying to exploit short term events for profits. For example, investors might target an earnings report or an anticipated product announcement.

Three ways to close an options contract

Now let's learn the three basic ways that you can close an options contract, now that we have some familiarity with the lingo.

- The option expires out of the money. That means that the option is worthless. You do nothing and move on. The seller of the option simply pockets the premium.

- The option expires in the money. In that case, it's up to the buyer to exercise their options. If they choose to, then the underlying stock is traded.

- The last option is to sell the option – i.e., trade it to someone else – prior to the expiration date. If you are losing money on the options contract, you can trade it and cut your losses now, rather than finding out what will happen if you hold it to the expiration date. On the other hand, if you are profiting from the option, you can sell it to get out now with profits.

Although we are spending a lot of time talking about exercising the option with the contract, options are only exercised in about 12% of trades. About 20%

expire as worthless contracts. The rest are bought and sold prior to the expiration date.

Reading Options Quotes

It's important to know how to read options quotes. Some have more information in them than others because some of the associated information is implied. First, let's look at this fictitious options quote:

ACMC AUGUST 12, 2019 120 CALL AT $2.50

- ACMC is the stock ticker. Our example is our fictitious company, Acme Communications.
- The date given is the expiration date of the option.
- 120 is the strike price, or $120.
- We're told it's a call option, or a bet the stock will increase in price.
- The final quoted price, $2.50, is the premium paid per share.

If an option is shaded in the online display, that means it's in the money. Options that are not shaded are out of the money.

Chapter 3: Strike Price

The strike price is one of the most important if not the most important thing to understand when it comes to option contracts. The strike price will determine whether the underlying stock is actually bought or sold at or before the expiration date. When evaluating any options contract, the strike price is the first thing that you should look at. It's worth reviewing the concept and how it's utilized in the actual marketplace.

The strike price will let you home in on the profits that can be made on an options contract. It's the break-even point but also gives you an idea as to your profits and losses. Of course, the seller always gets the premium no matter what.

For a call contract, the strike price is the price that must be exceeded by the current market price of the underlying equity. For example, if the strike price is $100 on a call contract, and the current market price goes to any price above $100, then the purchaser of the call can exercise their right at any time to buy the stock. Then the stock can be disposed of with a profit. Suppose that the current price rises to $130. Then you can exercise your option to buy the stock at $100 a share, and then turn around and sell it on the market for $130 a share, making a $30 profit per share before taking into account the premium and other fees that might accrue with your trades. While as the buyer of the contract you have no obligations other than paying the premium, the seller is obligated no matter what, and they must sell you the shares at $100 per share no matter how much it pains them to see the $130 per share price. Of course, there are reasons behind the curtain that will explain why they would bother entering this kind of arrangement that we will explore later.

For a put contract, the strike price likewise plays a central role, but the value of the stock relative to the strike price works in the opposite fashion. A put is a bet that the underlying equity will decrease in value by a certain amount. Hence if the stock price drops below the strike price, then the buyer can exercise their right to sell the shares at the strike price even though the market price is lower. So, if your price is $100, if the current price of the equity drops to $80, the seller obligated to buy the 100 shares per contract from you at $100 a share even though the market price is $80 per share. In this case, you've made a gross profit of $20 a share.

The value of the strike price will not only tell you profitability but give you an indication of how much the stock must move before you are able to exercise your rights. Often when the amount is smaller, you might be better off.

When you know the strike price of different options contracts, then you can evaluate which one is better for you to buy. Suppose that a stock is currently trading at $80 and you find two options put contracts. One has a strike price of $75 and the other has a strike price of $60. Further, let's suppose that both contracts expire at the same time. In the first case, the stock price in the market will need to drop just $5 before the contract becomes profitable. For the second contract, it will have to drop $20.

The potential worth of each contract per share is the difference. For the contract with the $75 strike price, that is only $5. For the second contract with the strike price of $60, the potential worth is $20, four times as much.

Determining which contract is better is a matter of analysis and taking some risk. You can't just go by face value, but you must take into consideration the expiration date together with an analysis of what the stock will actually do over that time period. It may be that it's going to be impossible for the stock to drop $20 in order to make the second contract valuable. If the expiration date comes before the stock drops that much in price, the contract will be worthless. In other words, you'd never be able to exercise your option of selling shares at strike amount. On the other hand, even though there is not much discrepancy between the strike and the market amount for the first contract, and the market price might only drop to say $70 per share, the chances of this happening before the expiration date is more likely.

Your analysis might be different if the contract with the lower strike price has a longer expiration date.

The lesson to take to heart is that a stock is more likely to move by smaller amounts over short time periods. But the higher the risk, the more the potential profits.

Chapter 4: Understanding the purchase of Options

Let's suppose that you're interested in buying shares in Acme Communications, and they are trading at $39 a share. To buy 100 shares, it would cost $3,900 plus brokerage/commission fees. For many people that is a lot of money to invest, and if you are a savvy investor, you might be more interested in purchasing options that you would be in laying out that much money per share. Keep in mind that our discussion below doesn't consider account brokerage commissions.

Suppose that instead you purchase an options contract and the price is $2.50. The premium is quoted on a per share basis, but an options contract is for 100 shares, so the total amount you will need to invest is 100 x $2.50 = $250.

Now suppose that you're bullish on the stock, and you settle on a strike price of $41. Let's say that on or before the expiration date the market price of Acme communications reaches $47.

Your gross profit per share is now $6. You've made $6 x 100 = $600. Subtracting the amount invested, not including commissions your profit is $600-$250 = $350. That's a return on investment of 140%.

If you had bought the shares, you could sell them at $47 a share for a profit of $800. While that is a bigger number in absolute terms, your return on investment would be about 21%.

Of course, depending on your financial situation, you aren't limited to purchasing one option contract. Remember that the stock was $39 a share, so if a person bought $3900 worth or 100 shares, they could have instead gone with 16 options contracts for $250 x 16 = $4,000. While the direct investor would have made their $800 profit, assuming that they sold when the price hit $47 a share, the options trader would have made $350 x 16 = $5,600 in profit (remember for both options – not considering commissions).

The downside is the risk that the stock price won't exceed the strike price. In that case, you're out the premium. If you had purchased 16 options contracts, then you'd be out the $4,000. The person who buys the stock won't be out nearly that much money. Let's say that the stock dropped to $37 a share. If they felt it would not be going anywhere anytime soon and they should sell at a loss, the person who bought the stocks would sell for $37 x 100 = $3700 and only be out $200 from their initial investment.

Using this example, you can see how investing in options contracts has a big upside in potential profits but also a bigger risk in losses. When you are talking about trading a single contract for 100 shares, the losses don't seem like a big deal, but you can see that going for more trades means that you're going to have to have a lot more awareness of the risks.

Of course, the options trader has one big advantage that the ordinary stock investor will never have, and that is the possibility of betting on the stock decreasing in value. Let's suppose that instead of dropping to $37 a share the stock dropped by $10 to $29 a share. So, 100 shares would be worth $2,900, and our investor friend would have lost $1,000 if they sell at that point.

Now let's say that instead of a call you invest in a put contract, the same scenario you buy 16 of them at $2.50, or $250 per contract. So, your total cost is again $4,000. This time say you have a strike price of $35. Your profit is $35-$29 = $6 per share.

This time you've made $9,600 ($6 per share, x 100 shares/contract x 16 contracts). With your initial investment, you've made a profit of $5,600 on the decline in stock price while your friend is nursing their losses. Again, you made a 140% ROI.

So, we see that buying options contracts can carry bigger risks while at the same time offering the potential for bigger rewards. In addition, they also offer the possibility of reaping the rewards when a stock drops in price, something that just isn't going to be possible with normal investing in stocks.

Chapter 5: Top Reasons to Trade Options

We've seen that trading options are an activity that has its upsides and its downsides. In this chapter, we are going to look at the top reasons that you want to trade options. Keep in mind that you can personalize your portfolio and investment strategy, so it's not necessary to go "all in" when it comes to trading options. You can have options trading as one part of a diverse investment strategy. In fact, many people use options to cover risks in other parts of their overall portfolio.

1. Trading Options provides an investment opportunity with limited capital

In the last chapter, we began with an example showing that for $250, you could control 100 shares of stock that would cost someone $3,900 to buy outright. We then expanded on that and saw what kind of possibilities existed when investing larger amounts. However, if you are just starting out with investing, it's not necessary to buy more than one options contract at a time. You can invest for a relatively small amount of money depending on the stock. Trading doesn't have to be approached with an all or nothing mentality. You can start with small investments and work your way up by reinvesting your profits.

2. You can hedge your risks with index funds

Most people who invest in stocks will be investing in index funds in order to have a diversified portfolio. By utilizing options, you can hedge your risks with index funds. Index puts can help you mitigate losses if the market experiences a major downturn. Smart investors will utilize index puts so that the next recession doesn't leave them with huge losses.

3. Profit off of other losses

OK, it sounds bad when phrased that way. But as we saw in the last chapter, you can use puts to profit from downturns in stock prices. This is an opportunity that simply isn't available when doing regular stock trading.

4. Collect Premiums

In the coming chapters, we'll investigate selling options contracts. As we'll see, there are ways to profit from doing so, but no matter what, you can pocket the premiums. This is another way to earn money in an overall investment portfolio that uses diverse strategies as well as diverse investments.

5. Capitalize on outsized gains

One of the biggest benefits that come with trading options is being able to control large amounts of stock that could have a huge upside if there is a major increase in stock price by purchasing a large number of call options. Of course, being a fortune teller isn't generally a lucrative income, but you can increase your chances of success by carefully studying the markets and the companies behind the individual stocks. Look for dynamic areas where new companies could see a huge gain in the stock price over a short period. The risk is that you'll lose your premium if the strike price isn't surpassed, but if it is then you'll have a chance to score big. In the previous chapter, we showed a simple example with a return on investment of 140%, but it's even possible to get an ROI of 500% or even more.

Chapter 6: Covered Calls

In this chapter, we'll investigate a trading strategy that is a good way to get started selling options for beginners. This strategy is called covered calls. By covered, we mean that you've got an asset that you own that covers the potential sale of the underlying stocks. In other words, you already own the shares of stocks. Now, why would you want to write a call option on stocks you already own? The basis of this strategy is that you don't expect the stock price to move very much during the lifetime of the options contract, but you want to generate money over the short term in the form of premiums that you can collect. This can help you generate a short-term income stream; you must structure your calls carefully.

Setting up covered calls is relatively low risk and will help you get familiar with many of the aspects of options trading. While it's probably not going to make you rich overnight, it's a good way to learn the tools of the trade.

Covered Calls involve a long position

In order to create a covered call, you need to own at least 100 shares of stock in one underlying equity. When you create a call, you're going to be offering potential buyers a chance to buy these shares from you. Of course, the strategy is that you're only going to sell high, but your real goal is to get the income stream from the premium.

The premium is a one-time non-refundable fee. If a buyer purchases your call option and pays you the premium, that money is yours. No matter what happens after that, you've got that cash to keep. In the event that the stock doesn't reach the strike price, the contract will expire, and you can create a new call option on the same underlying shares. Of course, if the stock price does pass the strike price, the buyer of the contract will probably exercise their right to buy the shares. You will still earn money on the trade, but the risk is you're giving up the potential to earn as much money that could have been earned on the trade.

You write a covered call option that has a strike price of $67. Suppose that for some unforeseen reason the shares skyrocket to $90 a share. The buyer of your call option will be able to purchase the shares from you at $67. So, you've gained $2 a share. However, you've missed out on the chance to sell the shares at a profit of $35 a share. Instead, the investor who purchased the call option from you will turn around and sell the shares on the markets for the actual spot price and they will reap the benefits.

However, you really haven't lost anything. You have earned the premium plus sold your shares of stock for a modest profit.

That risk – that the stocks will rise to a price that is much higher than the strike price - always exists, but if you do your homework, you're going to be offering stocks that you don't expect to change much in price over the lifetime of your call. So, suppose instead that the price only rose to $68. The price exceeded the strike price so the buyer may exercise their option. In that case, you are still missing out on some profit that you could have had otherwise, but it's a small amount and we're not taking into account the premium.

In the event that the stock price doesn't exceed the strike price over the length of the contract, then you get to keep the premium and you get to keep the shares. The premium is yours to keep no matter what.

In reality, in most situations, a covered call is going to be a win-win situation for you.

Covered Calls are a Neutral Strategy

A covered call is known as a "neutral" strategy. Investors create covered calls for stocks in their portfolio where they only expect small moves over the lifetime of the contract. Moreover, investors will use covered calls on stocks that they expect to hold for the long term. It's a way to earn money on the stocks during a period in which the investor expects that the stock won't move much at price and so have no earning potential from selling.

An Example of a Covered Call

Let's say that you own 100 shares of Acme Communications. It's currently trading at $40 a share. Over the next several months, nobody is expecting the stock to move very much, but as an investor, you feel Acme Communications has solid long-term growth potential. To make a little bit of money, you sell a call option on Acme Communications with a strike price of $43. Suppose that the premium is $0.78 and that the call option lasts 3 months.

For 100 shares, you'll earn a total premium payment of $0.78 x 100 = $78. No matter what happens, you pocket the $78.

Now let's say that over the next three months the stock drops a bit in price so that it never comes close to the strike price, and at the end of the three-month period, it's trading at $39 a share.

The options contract will expire, and it's worthless. The buyer of the options contract ends up empty-handed. You have a win-win situation. You've earned the extra $78 per 100 shares, and you still own your shares at the end of the contract.

Now let's say that the stock does increase a bit in value. Over time, it jumps up to $42, and then to $42.75, but then drops down to $41.80 by the time the options contract expires. In this scenario, you're finding yourself in a much better position. In this case, the strike price of $43 was never reached, so the buyer of the call option is again left out in the cold. You, on the other hand, keep the premium of $78, and you still get to keep the shares of stock. This time since the shares have increased in value, you're a lot better off than you were before, so it's really a win-win situation for YOU, even though it's a losing situation for the poor soul who purchased your call.

Sadly, there is another possibility, that the stock price exceeds the strike price before the contract expires. In that case, you're required to sell the stock. You still end up in a position that isn't all that bad, however. You didn't lose any actual money, but you lost a potential profit. You still get the premium of $78, plus the earnings from the sale of the 100 shares at the strike price of $43.

A covered call is almost a zero-risk situation because you never actually lose money even though if the stock price soars, you obviously missed out on an opportunity. You can minimize that risk by choosing stocks you use for a covered call option carefully. For example, if you hold shares in a pharmaceutical company that is rumored to be announcing a cure for cancer in two months, you probably don't want to use those shares for a covered call. A company that has more long-term prospects but probably isn't going anywhere in the next few months is a better bet.

How to go about creating a covered call

To create a covered call, you'll need to own 100 shares of stock. While you don't want to risk a stock that is likely to take off in the near future, you don't want to pick a total dud either. There is always someone willing to buy something – at the right price. But you want to go with a decent stock so that you can earn a decent premium.

You start by getting online at your brokerage and looking up the stock online. When you look up stocks online, you'll be able to look at their "option chain" which will give you information from a table on premiums that are available for calls on this stock. You can see these listed under bid price. The bid price is given on a per share basis, but a call contract has 100 shares. If your bid price is $1.75, then the actual premium you're going to get is $1.75 x 100 = $175.

An important note is that the further out the expiration date, the higher the premium. A good rule of thumb is to pick an expiry that is between two and three months from the present date. Remember that the longer you go, the higher the risk because that increases the odds that the stock price will exceed the strike price and you'll end up having to sell the shares.

You have an option (no pun intended) with the premium you want to charge. Theoretically, you can set any price you want. Of course, that requires a buyer willing to pay that price for you to actually make the money. A more reasonable strategy is to look at prices people are currently requesting for call options on this stock. You can do this by checking the asking price for the call options on the stock. You can also see prices that buyers are currently offering by looking at the bid prices. For an instant sale, you can simply set your price to a bid price that is already out there. If you want to go a little bit higher, you can submit the order and then wait until someone comes along to buy your call option at the bid price.

To sell a covered call, you select "sell to open."

Benefits of Covered Calls

- A covered call is a relatively low-risk option. The worst-case scenario is that you'll be out of your shares but earn a small profit, a smaller profit than you could have made if you had not created the call contract and simply sold your shares. However, you also get the premium.

- A covered call allows you to generate income from your portfolio in the form of premiums.

- If you don't expect any price moves on the stock in the near term and you plan on holding it long term, it's a reasonable strategy to generate income without taking much risk.

Risks of Covered Calls

- Covered calls can be a risk if you're bullish on the stock, and your expectations are realized, and there is a price spike. In that case, you've traded the small amount of income of the premium with a voluntary cap of the strike price for the potential upside you could have had if you had simply held the stock and sold it at the high price.

- If the stock price plummets, while you still get the premium, the stocks will be worthless unless they rebound over the long term. You shouldn't use a call option on stocks that you expect to be on the path to a major drop in the coming months. In that case, rather than writing a covered call, you should simply sell the stocks and take your losses. Alternatively, you can continue holding the stocks to see if they rebound over the long term.

Chapter 7: Buying Calls

Buying calls is a more advanced form of training than selling covered calls. But it's not that complicated, so let's dive in.

What you're actually buying

Remember that one option contract is for 100 shares, so you'll need to be able to buy 100 shares of the stock in order to exercise your right to buy.

Also, remember that an options contract has a deadline. If the stock price fails to exceed the strike price by the deadline, you're out of luck and will lose whatever money that you invested in the premium. In relative terms, the premium price will be small so chances are if you are careful and not starting out by buying large numbers of options contracts, you won't be out that much money.

Your Goal Buying Options Contracts

The goal when purchasing options contracts is to buy a stock at a price that is lower than its current market value. In other words, you want the stock price to be significantly higher than the strike price so that you're enjoying significant savings in purchasing the stock. When evaluating your options, you'll need to take into account the added costs of the premium paid plus commissions. In some cases, commissions can be substantial so make sure you know what they are ahead of time so that you choose a good strike price and exercise your options at the right time.

You're a trader, not an investor

You may be mentally conditioned to think in terms of investing. An investor wants to build a diversified portfolio over a long time period that they believe will increase in value over the long term. A trader operates in the same universe but has different goals. You are after short term profits – not investments. You are not going to hold this stock. If you were interested in holding the stock, you would simply buy it at the lower price that is currently on offer. Your goal is to be able to buy at the strike price when the stock has increased significantly in price and then sell it immediately so that you can pocket the profits.

Let's take an example. Suppose that XYZ corporation is currently selling at $30 a share. People are expecting the stock to rise, and some people are really bullish about its short-term prospects. If you are an investor, your goal is to get the stock at the lowest possible price and then hold it long term. If you are using strategies like dollar cost averaging, you might be buying a few shares every month without paying too much attention to what the price is specifically on the day you purchase. In any case, as an investor, you'll simply buy the shares at $30.

As a trader, you're hoping to cash in on the moves of XYZ over the next couple of months. You'll buy an options contract, let's say its premium is $0.90 and the strike price is $35. Your cost for the 100 shares is $90.

Then the stock price shoots up to $45. Since it passed the strike price, you can exercise your option to buy the shares at the strike price. You can buy them at $35 for a total price of $3,500. But remember – you're not an investor in for the long haul. You'll immediately unload the shares. You sell the shares for $4,500 and make a $1,000 profit. After considering your premium, your profit is $910. It will go a little bit lower after considering commissions, but you get the idea. The purpose of buying call options is to make fast profits on stocks you think are going to spike.

It's hard to guess when the best time is to really buy call options. Obviously, you don't want to do it when a major recession hit. The optimal time is during a bull market, or when a specific company is expected to hit on something big, that will suddenly increase its value in the markets. A good time to look is also when a recession hits, but it passes the bottom out period.

Benefits of Buying Call Options

Call options have many benefits that we've already touched on earlier. In Particular:

- Call options allow you to control 100 shares of stock without actually investing in the 100 shares – unless they reach a price where you get the profit that you want.

- Call options allow you to sit and wait, patiently watching the market before making your move.

- If your bet doesn't work out, you're only going to lose a small amount of money on the contract. In our example, if XYZ loses value, and ends up at $28 per share instead of moving past your strike price of $35, then you're only out the $90 you paid for the premium.

- Call buying provides a way to leverage expensive stock.

What to look for when buying Call options

Now let's take a look at some factors that you'll be on the lookout for when buying call options. You're going to want to be able to purchase shares of the stock you're interested in at a price that is less than the price you think it will go up to. You need to do this in order to ensure that the stock price surpasses the strike price. Of course, it's impossible to know what the future holds so this will involve a bit of speculation. You'll have to do a lot of reading and research to make educated guesses on where you expect the stock to go in the next few weeks or months.

Second, you'll need to take into account the cost of the premium when making your estimates. For the sake of simplicity, suppose that you find a call option with a premium of $1 per share. You're going to need a strike price that is high enough to take that into account. If you go for a stock that is $40 a share with a $1 premium and a strike price of $41, obviously you're not going to make anything unless the stock price goes higher than $41.

Remember that exercising your rights on the options contract is not a path toward immediate money. You're going to have to turn around and sell it ASAP in order to profit. Of course, when you sell is a judgment call as is when you exercise your right to buy. You're going to want to wait until the right moment to buy, but its impossible to really know what that right moment is. This is where trading experience helps and even then, the most skilled experts can make mistakes. For a beginner, the best thing to do is exercise your right to buy the shares and then sell them as soon as they've gone far enough past the strike price for you to make a profit and cover the premium. If you wait too long, there is always the chance that the stock price will start declining again, and it will go below your strike price and never exceed it again before the contract expires.

Open Interest

If you get online to check stocks you're interested in, one of the measures you will see is "Open Interest." This tells you the number of open or outstanding derivative contracts there are for that particular stock. Every time that a buyer and seller enter into an options contract, this value increases by one. What you want to do with open interest as a trader looking to make real cash from call options is to look for stocks that show big movement in the number of open trades. You're going to want to look for increasing numbers. This means that other traders have an interest in buying call options on this stock and that they're expecting it to go up in value in the near future.

Of course, you're going to want to take an educated approach to this. Simply getting online and going through random stocks will be a waste of time, it might take you weeks to find something.

You're going to want to prepare ahead of time by keeping an eye on the financial news. Watch Fox Business, read the Wall Street Journal, and watch CNBC and read any other financial publications that are to your liking. Find out what stocks the experts are talking about and which ones they expect to make significant moves over the next few weeks and months. Keep in mind these people and experts often make mistakes, so you're only using it as a guideline. You also don't want to focus solely on looking for stocks that are going to make moves; you want to keep up with company news. You need to keep your ears open for news such as the development of a new drug or the latest electronic gadget. Sometimes you might find out news about that before the stock begins attracting a lot of interest in the markets.

Tips for Buying Call Options

- Don't buy a call option with a strike price that you don't think the stock can beat.

- Always include the premium price in your analysis.

- Look for calls that are just in the money. These are likely to bring a modest profit.

- Call options that are out of the money might give you an option for a cheaper premium.

- However, the premium shouldn't be your primary consideration when looking to buy a call option. Compared to the money required to buy the shares and the potential profits if the stock goes past the strike price, the premium is going to be a trivial cost in most cases – provided of course the strike price is high enough to take the premium into account.

- Look at the time value. If you're looking for larger profits, it's better to aim for longer contracts. Remember, that with any call option you have the option to buy the stock at the strike price at any time between today's date and the deadline when the stock market price exceeds the strike price. Longer time frames mean you increase the chances of that happening. Even if the price goes a little above the strike price and dips down, with a longer window of time before the deadline, you can wait and see if it rebounds. Remember if it never does, you're only out the premium.

- Start small. Beginning traders shouldn't bet the farm on options. You'll end up broke if you do that. The better approach is to start by investing in one contract at a time and gaining experience as you go.

Chapter 8: Volatility in the Markets

While the stock market has long term trends that investors rely on fairly well as the years and decades go by, over the short term the stock market is highly volatile. By that, we mean that prices are fluctuating up and down and doing so over short time periods. Volatility is something that long-term investors ignore. It's why you will hear people that promote conservative investment strategies suggesting that buyers use dollar cost averaging. What this does is it averages out the volatility in the market. That way you don't risk making the mistake of buying stocks when the price is a bit higher than it should be, because you'll average that out by buying shares when it's a bit lower than it should be.

In a sense, over the short term, the stock market can be considered as a chaotic system. So from one day to the next, unless there is something specific on offer, like Apple introducing a new gadget that investors are going to think will be a major hit, you can't be sure what the stock price is going to be tomorrow or the day after that. An increase on one day doesn't mean more increases are coming; it might be followed by a major dip the following day.

For example, at the time of writing, checking Apple's stock price, on the previous Friday it bottomed out at $196. Over the following days, it went up and down several times, and on the most recent close, it was $203. The movements over a short-term period appear random, and to a certain extent, they are. It's only over the long term that we see the actual direction that Apple is heading.

Of course, Apple is at the end of a ten-year run that began with the introduction of the iPhone and iPad. It's a reasonable bet that while it's a solid long-term investment, the stock probably isn't going to be moving enough for the purposes of making good profits over the short term from trades on call options (not too mention the per share price is relatively high).

The truth is volatility is actually a friend of the trader who buys call options. But it's a friend you have to be wary of because you can benefit from volatility while also getting in big trouble from it.

The reason stocks with more volatility are the friend of the options trader is that in part the options trader is playing a probability game. In other words, you're looking for stocks that have a chance of beating the strike price you need in order to make profits. A volatile stock that has large movements has a greater probability of not only passing your strike price but doing so in such a fashion that it far exceeds your strike price enabling you to make a large profit.

Of course, the alternative problem exists – that the stock price will suddenly drop. That is why care needs to be a part of your trader's toolkit. A stock with a high level of volatility is just as likely to suddenly drop in price as it is to skip right past your strike price.

Moreover, while you're a beginner and might get caught with your pants down, volatile stocks are going to attract experienced options traders. That means that the stock will be in high demand when it comes to options contracts. What happens when there is a high demand for something? The price shoots up. In the case of call options, that means the stock will come with a higher premium. You will need to take the higher premium into account when being able to exercise your options at the right time and make sure the price is high enough above your strike price that you don't end up losing money.

Traders take some time to examine the volatility of a given stock over the recent past, but they also look into what's known as implied volatility. This is a kind of weather forecast for stocks. It's an estimate of the future price movements of a stock, and it has a large influence on the pricing of options. Implied volatility is denoted by the Greek symbol **σ,** implied volatility increases in bear markets, and it actually decreases when investors are bullish. Implied volatility is a tool that can provide insight into the options future value.

For options traders, more volatility is a good thing. A stock that doesn't have much volatility is going to be a stable stock whose price isn't going to change very much over the lifetime of a contract. So while you may want to sell a covered call for a stock with low volatility, you're probably not going to want to buy one if you're buying call options because that means there will be a lower probability that the stock will change enough to exceed the strike price so you can earn a profit on a trade. Remember too that stocks that are very volatile will attract a lot of interest from options traders and command higher premiums. You will have to do some balancing in picking stocks that are of interest.

Being able to pick stocks that will have the right amount of volatility so that you can be sure of getting one that will earn profits on short term trades is something you're only going to get from experience.

You should spend some time practicing before actually investing large amounts of money. That is, pick stocks you are interested in and make your bets but don't actually make the trades. Then follow them over the time period of the contract and see what happens. In the meantime, you can purchase safer call options, and so using this two-pronged approach gain experience that will lead to more surefire success down the road.

One thing that volatility means for everyone is that predicting the future is an impossible exercise. You're going to have some misses no matter how much knowledge and experience you gain. The only thing to aim for is to beat the market more often than you lose. The biggest mistake you can make is putting your life savings into a single stock that you think is a sure thing and then losing it all.

Options to pursue if your options aren't working

At this point, you may think that if the underlying stock for your option doesn't go anywhere or it tanks that you have no choice but to wait out the expiration date and count the money you spend on your premiums as a loss. That really isn't the case. The truth is, you can sell a call option you've purchased to other traders in the event its not working for you. Of course, you're not going to make a profit taking this approach in the vast majority of cases. But it will give you a chance to recoup some of your losses. If you have invested in a large number of call options for a specific stock and it's causing you problems, you need to recoup at least some of your losses may be more acute. Of course, the right course of action in these cases is rarely certain, especially if the expiration date for the contract is relatively far off in the future, which could mean that the stock has many chances to turn around and beat your strike price. Remember, in all bad scenarios actually buying the shares of stock is an option – you're not required to do it. In all cases, the biggest loss you're facing is losing the entire premium. You'll also want to keep the following rule of thumb in mind at all times – the more time value an option has, the higher the price you can sell the option for. If there isn't much time value left, then you're probably going to have to sell the option at a discount. If there is a lot of time value, you may be able to recoup most of your losses on the premium.

Let's look at some specific scenarios.

- The stock is languishing. If the stock is losing time value (that is getting closer to the expiration date) and doesn't seem to be going anywhere, you can consider selling the call option in order to recoup some of your losses related to the premium. The more time value, the less likely it is that selling the option is a good idea. Of course, the less time value, the harder it's going to be to actually sell your option. Or put another way, in order to actually sell it you're going to have to take a lower price.

- Suppose the stock isn't stagnant, but it's tanking. If there is a lot of time value left *and* there is some reason to believe that the company is going to make moves before the expiration date of your contract that will improve the fortunes of the stock when you can still profit from it, then you may want to ride out the downturn. This is a risky judgment call, and it's going to be impossible to know for sure what the right answer is, but you can make an educated guess. On the other hand, if the stock is tanking and there is no good news about the company on the horizon, you are pretty much facing the certainty that you're not going to be able to exercise your options to buy the shares. In that case, you should probably look at selling the option contract to someone more willing to take the risk. At least you can get some of the money back that you paid for the premium.

Now let's briefly consider the positive scenario. Buying options and then trading the stocks can feel like a roller coaster ride, and that rush is what attracts a lot of people to options trading besides the possibilities of making short term profits. Let's consider an example where the stock keeps rising in price? How long do you wait before selling?

There are two risks here. The first risk is that you're too anxious to sell and so do it at the first opportunity. That really isn't a huge downside; you're going to make some profits in that case. On the other hand, it's going to be disconcerting when you sit back and watch the stock continuing to rise. That said, this is better than some of the alternatives.

One of the alternatives is waiting too long to buy and sell the shares. You might wait and see the stock apparently reaching a peak, and then get a little greedy hoping that it's going to keep increasing so you can make even more profits. But then you keep waiting, and suddenly the stock starts dropping. Maybe you wait a little more hoping it's going to start rebounding and going up again, but it doesn't, and you're forced to buy and sell at a lower price than you could have gotten. Maybe it's even dropping enough so that you lose your opportunity altogether. A really volatile stock might suddenly crash, leaving you with a lost opportunity.

The reality is that like everything else involved in options trading since none of us can see the future it's going to be flat out impossible to know if you are making the right call every single time. Keep in mind that your goal is to make a profit on your trades. Don't get greedy about it, hoping for more riches than you actually see on the screen. In other words, the goal isn't to sell at maximum possible profits. Nobody knows what those are because it's going to be virtually impossible to predict what price the stock will peak at before the contract expires. Instead, you're going to want to focus on making an acceptable profit. Before you even buy your call options, you should sit down and figure out a reasonable range of values that define ahead of time what that acceptable profit level is. Then when the stock price hits your target range, you exercise your options and sell the shares. You take your profit and move on, going to the next trades.

That is not a guarantee that you're going to make money on every trade, but it's a more rules-based system that gets you into the mindset of trading based on objective facts rather than relying on unbridled emotions.

Also, remember that you can exercise the option to buy the shares, and then hold them until you think you've reached the right moment to sell. At other times, you may want to exercise the option to buy shares and hold in your portfolio as a long-term investment.

Chapter 9: In the money, out of the money

When trading options you're often going to hear the terms in the money and out of the money. We've defined them but lets briefly take a closer look at what they mean.

In the Money

In the money simply means that exercising the option would result in a profit. For a call option, that means that the current stock price has risen above the strike price.

If Acme Communications is trading at $100 a share, and you have a call option with a strike price of $60, that means that you're in the money and you can buy the shares at $60 and sell them for $100 in the market. The option contract is said to have an intrinsic value that is equal to the difference between the stock price and the strike price, that is $100-$60 = $40 is the intrinsic value.

When you automatically exercise your options

If you have enough cash in your brokerage account when the call option contract expires to cover the purchase of the underlying shares at the strike price, if the call option expires in the money, then you're going to purchase the stocks automatically. Of course, you can sell them right away for a profit or hold them, your choice at that point.

Out of the Money

When the strike price is higher than the market price of the underlying asset, the call option is said to be out of the money. A call option that is out of the money has no intrinsic value, but it may have time value. Any option that reaches the expiry is worthless if it's out of the money at that point. However, if it still has time value and the underlying asset has been increasing in value such that the option is closer to being in the money, then it may be valuable enough to sell the option to another investor, and they may purchase it from you at a higher price than you paid for the premium. So, remember here that we are talking about trading the option itself, and not the underlying stock. So if you sell the option to someone else, you may recoup all or part of the premium, or even make a profit on it, however, the investor who buys it from you will be the one who can exercise the right to buy the stocks and/or hold the option until the expiration date.

Chapter 10: Buying and Selling Puts

So far, we've talked exclusively about buying and selling call options. Generally speaking, this is a better option for beginning traders. Our belief is that starting out selling covered call options, then moving on to limited purchases of call options is the best way to get started in options trading. Once you gain experience in that, you can move on to trading options themselves and also with buying and selling put options.

Let's quickly review what's involved in puts. A put is a bet on a decrease in stock price. Truthfully, puts aren't really all that different than calls, because a call is based on an educated hunch that some stock is going to go up in price in the coming weeks or months. A put is a bet that the opposite will occur, in other words, that the stock market price is going to decrease in the coming weeks or months.

First, let's look at how in-the-money and out-of-the-money are defined for puts.

How a Put Option Works

A put option from the buyer's perspective is the option to sell the underlying stock asset at a pre-agreed strike price. In this case, the bet you're making as the buyer of the contract is that the stock price is going to drop in value, and then you can sell the shares to the seller of the put contract at a higher price.

Suppose there is a pharmaceutical company called Theran Nose. Let's say that the shares are currently trading at $100, but there is bad news swirling around. You've studied the situation and are confident the stock will fall and do so more than dropping to $70. You find a seller of a put contract that doesn't think it's going to drop that much by the expiration date, and so they sell you the put option with a $70 strike price.

Then a week before the expiration date, the price crashes to $40 a share. In the case of a put, the seller of the put MUST purchase the shares from you. So, you buy the stock at $40 a share, and then you sell the shares to the seller at $70 a share. Needless to say, they will be seriously irritated, but you made a better bet and come out with a profit of $30 a share.

In the Money

In the case of a put option, when the stock price is below the strike price, it is said to be in the money. If the strike price is $150, and the stock price is $100, the put option has an intrinsic value of $50. The buyer of the put can buy the stock at $100 a share and sell it for $150 a share.

Out of the money

In the case of a put, if the market price is above the strike price, then there is no intrinsic value. In an analogous fashion to that we've seen for call options, however, if the contract has time value, then it may still be possible to profit from the contract. You may be able to sell it to another investor and get some or all of your premium back, or if there is enough time value, and it looks like even though the stock has yet to decline below the strike price that there are decent odds that it will, then you might get lucky and find an investor who will buy the option contract from you.

Using Puts as Insurance

So far, we've talked about put options in terms of speculating. That is, over the short-term interval of the contract, you believe that the underlying stock is going to drop in price and do so by dropping below the strike price. However, a put option can also be used as a form of insurance for securities in your portfolio. This can work for index funds or for individual stocks.

Suppose you have a stock that you're hoping to hold for the long term. Its prospects are uncertain, so there is a chance that you could lose a lot of money. Maybe you've invested in 1,000 shares. If you do nothing and the stock tanks, then you're out of luck. For the sake of example, we'll say that you bought the stock at $10 a share, for a total price of $10,000. Then after some bad news, it tanks, dropping to $2 a share. Now you're left with an investment worth just $2,000, and you lost $8,000. Your only hope is to either sell now and cut your losses or hold it and hope that things get better in the future.

Another alternative is to buy some put contracts on the stock. Let's say the contracts have a premium of $0.56, so it costs $56 to buy a put contract for 100 shares. Altogether, you'll have to invest $560 to buy enough to cover your entire investment.

Now suppose that they came with a strike price of $7.

The stock tanks to $2 a share. You can then sell your shares at $7 to the seller of the puts. That gives you $7,000 back. Incorporating the cost of the premium, you've recovered $6,440.

Although you haven't recovered all of your losses, it's certainly true that having $6,440 is far better than only being able to recoup $2,000. We see how a put acting as an insurance policy can help protect our existing investments.

Speculating with Puts

Speculating with puts is trickier than doing so with call options. In fact, the most famous options traders are those who "short" a stock, and there is a good reason. Knowing which stocks are going to fall might seem obvious, but it doesn't always work that way. Without getting inside information, which of course is illegal, you're going to have to make educated guesses. In other words, the advice here is basically the same as it is with calls. You'll have to study the markets and watch all the financial news networks to find out what companies have prospects for heading into a downturn. Overall, of course, a bear market or recession will be the best time to look for a prospect for put options.

Chapter 11: Beginners Common Mistakes

Trading options are more involved than trading stocks, so there are ample opportunities to make mistakes. It's important to take the approach of going small and slow at first so that you don't lose the shirt off your back. That said, if you run into mistakes don't get too down about it. Dust yourself off and get up to fight another day. With that said, let's have a look at some common mistakes and how to avoid them.

Putting all your eggs in one basket

While there is a difference between investing and trading, as traders can learn a few things from our investor brothers (and most people are a little of both anyway). Don't let everything ride on one trade. If you take all the money you have and invest it in buying options for one stock, you're making a big mistake. Doing that is very risky, and as a beginning trader, you're going to want to mitigate your risk as much as possible. Betting on one stock may pay off sometimes, but more times than not it's going to lead you into bankruptcy territory.

Investing more than you can

It's easy to get excited about options trading. The chances to make fast money and the requirements that you analyze the markets can be very enticing. Oftentimes that leads people into getting more excited than they should. A good rule to follow with investing is to make sure that you're setting aside enough money to cover living expenses every month, with a security fund for emergencies. Don't bet the farm on some sure thing by convincing yourself that you'll be able to make back twice as much money and so cover your expenses. Things don't always work out.

Going all in before you're ready

Another mistake is failing to take the time to learn options trading in real time. Just like getting overly excited can cause people to bet too much money or put all their money on one stock, some people are impatient and don't want to take the time to learn the options markets by selling covered calls. It's best to start with covered calls and then move slowly to small deals buying call options. Leave put options until you've gained some experience.

Failure to study the markets

Remember, you need to be truly educated to make good options trades. That means you'll need to know a lot about the companies that you're either trying to profit from or that you're shorting. Options trading isn't possible without some level of guesswork, but make your guesses educated guesses, and don't rely too much on hunches.

Not Getting Enough Time Value

Oftentimes, whether you're trading puts or calls, the time value is important. A stock may need an adequate window of time in order to beat the stock price whether it's going above it or plunging below it. When you're starting out and don't know the markets as well as a seasoned trader, you should stick to options you can buy that have a longer time period before expiring.

Not having adequate liquidity

Sometimes beginning investors overestimate their ability to play the options markets. Remember that if you buy an option, to make it work for you-you're going to need money on hand to buy stocks when the iron is hot. And you're going to need to buy 100 shares for every option contract. Before entering into the contract, make sure that you're going to be able to exercise your option.

Not having a grip on volatility

If you don't understand volatility and its relation to premium pricing, you may end up making bad trades.

Failing to have a plan

Trading seems exciting, and when you're trading, you may lose the investors mentality. However, traders need to have a strategic plan as much as investors do. Before trading, make sure that you have everything in place, including knowing what your goals are for the trades, having pre-planned exit strategies, developing criteria for getting into a trade so that you're not doing on a whim or based on emotion.

Ignoring Expiration Dates

It sounds crazy, but many beginners don't keep track of the expiration date. Would you hate to see a stock go up in price, and then hope it keeps going up, and it does, only to find out that your expiration date passed before you exercised your option?

Overleveraging

It's easy to spend huge amounts of money in small increments. This is true when it comes to trading options. Since stocks are more expensive, it's possible to get seduced by purchasing low priced options. After all, options are available at a fraction of the cost that is required to buy stocks. And you might keep on purchasing them until you're overleveraged.

Buying cheap options

In many cases, buying cheap things isn't a good strategy. If you're buying a used car, while you might occasionally find a great car that is a good buy, in most cases a car is cheap for a reason. The same applies to options trading. When it comes to options, a cheap premium probably denotes the option is out of the money. Sure, you save some money on a cheap premium, but when the expiration date comes, you might see the real reason the option contract was a cheap buy. Of course, as we described earlier, there may be cases where cheap options have the capacity to rebound and become profitable by the time the expiry date arrives. But taking chances like that is best left to experienced traders.

Giving in to panic

Remember that you have the right to buy or sell a stock if you've purchased an option. Some beginners panic and exercise their right far too early. This can happen because of fears that they'll be missing out an opportunity with a call option, or because of fears that a stock won't keep going down on a put.

Not Knowing how much cash you can afford to lose

Going into options trading blindly is not a smart move. With each option trade you make, you need to have a clear idea of how much cash you have on hand to cover losses and exercising your options. You'll also want to know how much cash you can afford to lose if things go south.

Jumping into puts without enough experience and cash to cover losses

Remember if you're selling puts, you will have to buy the stock at the strike price if the buyer exercises their option. This is a huge risk. The stock could have plunged in value, and you're going to have to buy the stock at the strike price, possibly leaving you with huge losses. Don't go into selling puts with your eyes closed, in fact, beginners are better off avoiding selling puts.

But if you must do it, make sure you can absorb the losses when you bet wrong.

Piling it on

Most beginner mistakes are related to panic. If you're looking at losses on options, some beginners double and triple up hoping to make it up when things turn better. Instead, they end up losing more money. Instead of giving in to panic, learn when to cut your losses and re-evaluate your trading strategy.

Staying in a written contract when you should get out

If you've sold an option and it's looking like you might face a loss, you can always get out of it by selling.

Chapter 12: Advanced Trading Strategies

In this chapter, we'll look at some advanced trading strategies.

Long Straddle

In a long straddle, you'll simultaneously buy a put and call for the same underlying stock. You're also going to want the same strike price and expiration date. This technique is something that can be utilized with a highly volatile stock. That way you have the possibility of profiting no matter which way the stock moves. Before we see how this works, let's step back for a second and recall how we determine whether or not a deal is going to be profitable. We are looking at this from the buyer's perspective.

In a call option, you're going to profit when the stock exceeds the strike price. However, you must remember to include the premium in your calculation.

If you think a stock will go higher than $54, but you're paying a $1 premium per share, then you will have to invest in a call option that has a strike price of at least $55.

In a put option, it's the same game, but you're hoping the stock will go below the strike price. So, for our new scenario of buying a call and a put at the same strike price and expiration date, we will buy a put with a strike price of $55. For simplicity, we will stay with a $1 premium.

Now you need to know the net premium, which will be the sum of the premium from the call option + the premium from the put option, in this case, $2.

You can get a profit when one of two conditions are met:

- Price of underlying stock > (Strike price of call + Net Premium). In our example, you will make a profit when the amount of the underlying stock is higher than $55 + $2 = $57.

- Price of underlying stock < (Strike price of put – Net Premium). Using our example, you'll see a profit when the price of the underlying stock is less than $55- $2 = $53.

The maximum loss for a straddle will occur when the contract expires with the underlying trading at the strike price. In that case, both contracts expire, and you're out the premiums paid for both options.

A long straddle has two break-even points. These are:

- Lower breakeven point: Strike price – Net premium
- Upper breakeven point: Strike price + Net premium

Remember you buy both options with the same strike price and expiration date.

Let's look at a simple example. A stock is trading at $100 a share in May. The investor buys a call with a strike price of $200 that expires on the third Friday in June for $100. The investor also buys a put with a strike price of $200 that expires on the third Friday of June for $100.

The net premium is $100 + $100 = $200.

Now suppose that on the expiry date, the stock is trading at $300. The put expires as worthless since the stock price of the underlying is far above the strike price of the put. However, the investor's call option expires in the money with an intrinsic value of 100 x ($300 - $200) = $10,000. Less the premium the investor has made $9,800.

On the other hand, suppose that the stock drops in value, and on the expiry is trading at $50. This time, the call option expires as worthless. The investor can buy 100 shares at a price of $50 each for a total cost of $5,000. Now he can sell them to exercise the put option at $200 a share, so he nets $20,000 - $5,000 - $200 = $14,800.

This is a fictitious example, so whether the numbers are realistic or not really isn't the point – the point is that the investor will profit no matter what happens to the stock price.

Strangle

The term strangle is an adaptation of the straddle. In this case, you also simultaneously buy a call option and a put option. However, instead of buying them at the same strike price, you buy them at different strike prices. For this type of strategy, you will buy slightly out-of-money options. This is used when you think that the underlying stock will undergo significant volatility in the short term. You will achieve a profit with a strangle when one of two conditions are met:

- Price of underlying stock > (strike price of call + Net Premium paid) or

- Price of underlying stock < (strike price of put – Net premium paid)

Usually, the strike price of the put is set at a lower value. Profit is determined by one of two possibilities:

- Profit = Price of underlying stock – strike price of call – net premium
- Profit = Strike price of put– the price of underlying stock – net premium

Bear Spread

A bear spread is profitable when the underlying stock price declines. Like the above strategies, a bear spread involves the simultaneous purchase of more than one option; however, in a bear spread, you buy two options of the same type. Alternatively, a call bear spread involves selling a call with a low strike price and buying a call with a high strike price.

Bull Spread

A bull spread is designed to profit when the price of the underlying security has a modest price increase. You can do a bull spread using either call or put options.

Married Puts

A married put is basically an insurance policy like that we described earlier. You buy a stock and a put option at the same time, in order to protect yourself against possible losses from the stock.

Cash Secured Puts

In a cash-secured put, you secure the possible purchase of stock by having money in your brokerage account to cover the purchase. This will allow you to purchase stock at a discount, provided you have enough money in your account to actually buy the stock. In short, you write a put option and set aside the cash to purchase the stock. Cash secured put is done when you are bullish on the underlying stock but believe it will undergo a temporary downturn.

Rolling

Rolling a trade simply means that you are simultaneously closing out your existing positions and opening new ones based on the same underlying stock. When rolling a position, you can change the strike price, the duration of the contract, or both. You can roll forward, which means to extend the expiration date for the option.

A roll-up means that you increase the strike price when you open the new contract. A roll-up is used on a call option when you believe the underlying stock is going to increase in price. When you are trading put options, you use a roll down. In that case, you close your option and reopen it with the same underlying stock but with a lower strike price. A higher strike price means that the new position will be cheaper. When rolling, you're going out in time to deadline. When rolling a call, you're hoping that the stock will rise in price. In this case, you're rolling to an out of the money position. The price of the new call will drop.

With a put, the opposite occurs, and the price of the new put will increase.

Conclusion

Thank you for taking the time to read this book. If you have found this book useful as a tool for your investment education, please take a moment to jump on Amazon and offer an honest review. We sincerely hope that the information contained herein will help you grow and learn how to invest more wisely and realize greater profits.

Many investors are struck with fear at the mere mention of options trading. Derivatives are a mysterious concept that harkens visions of the 2008 financial collapse. This is the kind of brainwashing that we constantly receive from financial experts (who don't want you intruding on their secret games) and from friends, family, and media, who have left us conditioned so that we are too risk averse. The fact is if you understand the markets, options trading is not nearly as dangerous as it's made out to be. Moreover, it's far more exciting and interesting than taking the completely safe and boring path, investing in mutual funds or just letting the money sit inside your 401k.

While this book certainly does not cover everything, you need to know about options, as it's an introductory book that only scratches the surface, you have enough foundational knowledge to begin your foray into the world of options trading. We hope that you will approach your trading activities sensibly. This means that while you're going to be more willing to assume risk than someone locked into mutual funds, or simply buying and holding stocks from the stock market, that you will still take a reasonable and conservative approach to trade. We advise new traders to start slowly, focusing on one type of trade and growing as they gain experience and confidence. Stay conservative as you begin by writing call options for stocks that you already own so that you can benefit from the premium income while not taking much real risk. If you follow this path, even if you do end up losing your shares, you'll do so at a modest profit. That gives you the opportunity to load up and do it again and keep repeating the process until you've achieved mastery. As you gain experience, then you'll be able to move on to more ambitious types of trading and hopefully larger profits.

The first time that you start seeing profits rolling in from your options trading, you'll feel a tinge of excitement that let's be honest – few people actually experience these days. Remember to review not only the best techniques used but go over the beginner's mistakes so that you'll reduce the chances that you'll be the person making them. And most importantly, please remember that this book is only a starting point. You'll want to read my other books and also use them as a springboard to more advanced and detailed treatments. Best of luck and many profits in your trading activities!

Introduction

Welcome to How to Trade Options: Day Trading Strategies!

In this book, we will look at using Day Trading in the exciting world of options to help you build your wealth fast. If you're interested in options, you'll probably also want to check out my other books on the How to Trade Options series, in particular "How to Trade Options" which covers beginner topics in detail.

Day Trading is a fun and active way to participate in the markets and take advantage of the short-term ups and downs that provide profit opportunities. It's far more challenging than stocks and requires a deeper knowledge of the markets when compared to the casual investor or even that many financial advisors, who are focused on the long term, possess. But don't let that intimidate you! Day trading and being successful at is an accessible skill, provided you're willing to take the time to study companies and the markets and stay on top of the news the way you'll need to in order to succeed.

Day Trading also carries some risk with it, more risk as compared to normal stock trading or even trading options in the usual way. I advise you to get into day trading using capital that you can afford to lose. But despite common perceptions that the stock market is some kind of gambling casino, it is anything but. You'll approach your trades using reasoned analysis, which will strongly tip the odds in your favor. But you do need to be aware of the risk is real.

We'll begin by reviewing options, so you are reminded about what they are and how they work, but this book isn't aimed at beginners. See my first book on the topic How to Trade Options for more details.

After that, we'll learn how day trading works, and then apply it to using options to make money over short time periods. Best of luck in the markets!

Chapter 1: Options – the Basics

Most people who invest in the stock markets do so with the desire to have safe investments that will grow over the long term of 5,10 and even 30 years. Others prefer a more active approach that lets them make money over shorter time intervals, even weeks. Or they want a hedge, neutral strategies, or even the ability to bet against a company in the belief its stock will decline. All of this action takes place in the options market, which is an exciting way to take a more active interest in stocks. Before we look at day trading, we will provide a quick review of the concepts of options.

What is an option

An option is simply a contract between two parties which is based on an underlying asset. You can create an options contract for any type of asset, but our focus is on options contracts for stocks. They are called *options* because one party of the contract will have the option to buy or sell stocks depending on whether or not certain conditions are met.

An option is a type of *derivative*. While they've been around for a long time, the general public really didn't become aware of the concept of derivatives until the 2008 financial crash, when a particular type of derivative, mortgage-backed securities, caused financial havoc when huge numbers of bets went bad at the same time. A derivative, sounds fancy but all it means is that it's an asset whose value depends on the value of something else. In the case of options, the options contract is based on the value of the shares of stocks that the contract is based on.

One option contract represents 100 shares of stock. The contract will cost the buyer a much smaller sum than it would cost to buy the shares of stock. In a sense, an options contract is a bet that the stock will move in a certain direction over a given time period. That is why they can be used for speculation. Like most contracts, an options contract has an expiration date or "expiry". In the United States options can be exercised on or before the expiration date, if the agreed-upon condition is realized. In Europe, they can only be exercised on the expiration date.

There are, of course, only two ways a stock can move, and so there are two types of options contracts. These are:

- A call: this is a bet that the stock will rise in price on or before the ending date of the contract.
- A put: this is a bet that the stock will decline in price, on or before the ending date of the contract.

For a call, the condition that the contract is based on is that the price of a share of stock will go up past an agreed upon price per share, which is called the *strike price*. When it does, the buyer of the option can exercise their right to buy the shares of stock from the seller (or writer as they are called) of the call option. That is, they can "call it in". If the share price goes above the strike price, the writer or seller of the call contract *must* sell the shares if the buyer chooses to exercise their right to buy them.

This is true no matter how high the stock price has risen. So, suppose that the strike price for ABC stock was set at $67 when the contract was entered into by the two parties. Second, we'll assume that at that time the share price was $65. If the share price rises to $68 a share, the owner of the shares must sell them if the buyer wants to exercise their option (to buy the shares). This is also true if the share price rises to $100.

The seller of the contract takes a bit of risk. They can't lose money, but they might miss out on a big move in the share price of the stock, and hence miss out on a big profit they could have had.

Why bother? The reason is that the buyer can buy the shares at the strike price. If the shares have risen to $100 a share, the buyer can buy the shares from the seller of the options contract at $68 per share, and then immediately turn around and sell them for $100 a share, making a quick profit of $32 per share! Of course, that is a quote of gross revenue, there are some fees involved and a commission to the broker, but in the end, the buyer would make a substantial profit in this scenario.

Now you may be wondering why the person selling the contract would bother. The reason is that they can charge a non-refundable fee for entering into the contract. This fee is called *the premium*. If you're selling calls, you get to keep the premium no matter what. In many cases, the share price will never exceed the strike price, so they get to keep the premium and the shares. In the event that it does exceed the strike price, they get to keep the premium, and even though they may have missed out on some profit they could have had, they will probably earn a bit of profit on the shares they sold anyway. For the seller, it's a win-win deal. This kind of option contract is known as a *covered call*.

Covered calls provide one option strategy, which is to generate income from your shares.

Premiums are small, as compared to the price of the underlying stock. The risk to the buyer of the call is relatively small, and they get the chance to control shares of stock for a certain time without actually owning them. Of course, to exercise your option, you will have to have the capital on hand or access to the capital in order to buy the shares to make your quick profit. Many people, however, don't even do that and they simply trade options (that is you get the contract, and then sell it on the options markets before the expiry).

Options contracts are for 100 shares each. Premiums will usually be pretty small, so say $1 per share, so you can buy the options contract for 100 shares for $100. If it doesn't work out for the buyer, they lose a relatively small amount of money, as compared to the large funds that would be involved actually buying the stock. From the buyers perspective, it gives them the ability to speculate on the markets for relatively small sums of money and without actually owning the stock. Then if their speculation proves right, they can exercise their options and buy and sell the shares of stock.

When you read about options, they are typically described in some fancy sounding language. It will make sense now that you've seen how a covered call works. For a call, an option is a contract giving the owner the right, but not the obligation, to buy shares of stock at a fixed price over a specific, limited time period. Typically, options contracts last a few months, but you can also buy *weeklys*, which last a week on Fridays. There are also *quarterly* which expire the last business day at the end of each quarter. Also, for long term considerations, you can buy LEAPS which is typically a time period over a few years.

Now let's take a look at the other type of options contract, which is known as a *put*. A put gives the buyer the right to sell the underlying stock at an agreed-upon price on or before the expiration date. Again, the put contract is sold for a premium and the pre-agreed upon share price is known as the strike price. When a trader buys a put, the bet is that the price of the stock will go below the strike price over the lifetime of the contract. Let's illustrate with an example.

Joe buys a put contract for XYZ Company. At the time that he buys the put contract, XYZ is trading at $100 a share. The premium for the contract is $2, so he buys it for $200. The strike price is $90.

Joe believes or has heard that some bad news will come out about XYZ, or maybe he is simply bearish about the market at large. Then before the contract expires, the bad news does come out. The share price drops to $60. Now Joe can exercise his right in the contract.

He buys 100 shares on the stock market at $60 a share. The seller of the put contract *must* buy the shares from Joe – at the strike price. So, the seller buys 100 shares of XYZ stock at $90 a share, and Joe walks away with a $30 per share profit (less the premium fee and brokerage commission).

The seller of the put got a raw deal, they probably doubted the news would drive the stock price that low, and so made a bet it wouldn't in order to get the income from the premium. Even though they lost their bet they get to keep the premium, so they aren't totally out. They also have the 100 shares of XYZ, and who knows, maybe things will turn around in the future.

These are dramatic examples designed for illustration. Most of the time stock probably won't move that much, although options traders try to look for volatile stocks that are moving a lot. Sellers will probably try and sell more stable stocks, so they won't risk as much.

If the share price of stock never goes above the strike price in the case of a call or goes below the share price in the case of a put by the expiration date, the option expires worthless. The seller of the option walks away with their premium and in the case of the call, keeps their shares, and in the case of a put, has no obligation to buy shares. The buyer of the option loses only the premium when the option expires worthless (note that the buyer never gets the premium back under any circumstances).

Trading Options

Now like anything else, you can buy and sell an option itself. What is an option worth? The premium! Depending on various factors, the premium can go up or down. The person who buys the options contract is the owner of the contract. The seller still has their obligation, if the share price meets the required conditions against the strike price in the contract.

The owner of the option is considered to be *long* in the position. If you are short on the position, that means you've sold an option you didn't own at the time of sale.

The buyer of an option has three possible outcomes:

- They can hold the option until it expires, and the strike price is not exceeded, so the option expires worthless.
- They can sell the option at some point before it expires. In this case, you are said to "close out your position".
- They can exercise their rights under the option. This means you will buy the underlying shares of stock or sell the underlying shares of stock, for a call or a put, respectively.

The buyer of the option is the person with the right but not the obligation to buy or sell the shares. The seller of the option contract (also sometimes called the writer) has an obligation to buy or sell the shares. Their possible outcomes are:

- You can buy the option back and close out your position.

- Take "assignment", which means buy or sell the shares as required if they have met the condition set by the strike price.
- If the strike price condition isn't met, you let the contract expire worthlessly, and keep your premium.

Of course, remember that in all cases the seller always keeps the original premium.

An option can be *in the money* or *out of the money*. If an option for ABC stock has a strike price of $50 and shares of ABC stock are trading for $55, the option is in the money $5. If the shares are trading for $47, the option is out of the money $3.

For a call, it works in the opposite way, since you earn money as the buyer of the option if the stock falls below the strike price. For ABC, a put option with a strike price of $50, if the stock price is trading at $55, the option is out of the money $5. On the other hand, for a put contract, if it's trading at $40, the option contract is in the money $10.

The *intrinsic value* of an option is the amount that it is in the money.

We also need to know the so-called *time value* of the option. This is the difference between the intrinsic value and the premium per share paid for the option. That is:

Time value = premium paid – value in the money

If you paid $7 for an XYZ option and it's in the money $2, the time value is $7 - $2 = $5.

When an option is out of the money, it has no intrinsic value. So the time value is given by the premium paid, but it declines at increasing rates as the expiration date gets closer. In other words, the options contract will be worth less and less to a potential buyer since its likely to expire worthlessly.

When you look at an options ticker, it will include the premium (the cost of buying on a per share basis) and the expiration date. Options also have a *deliverable*, which is the amount of the underlying that will be bought or sold if the option is exercised. Typically, this is 100 shares of the stock. The *multiplier* defines the net credit or debit to your account if the option is exercised (or assigned, in the case that you are the writer of the option).

A few more things to be aware of as a buyer include:

- Break-even point: This is the strike price + option premium.
- Maximum loss: Premium paid for the option.

Long vs. Short

There are four basic options available:

- Long call: this is the right to buy shares. An example would be buying a covered call option as described earlier. This means you are bullish on the stock, that is you expect its value to increase, possibly by a large amount.

- Long put: this is the right to sell shares of stock. You're bearish on the stock, but it's long because you expect to profit from the options contract by being able to sell the shares at the strike price which is higher than the share price on the market.

- Short call: An obligation to sell a stock. You're bearish on the stock, and don't believe the share price will increase enough to beat the strike price. It can be covered, meaning that you already own the shares (lower risk) or naked, which means you don't own the shares when you write the contract (high-risk trade).

- Short put: This is an obligation to buy shares of stock. You're bullish on the stock and believe the share price will stay above the strike price.

Now let's size up potential profits and losses for the different options.

Long Call (role: buyer)

For our long call, let's assume we have:

Long 1 ABC Aug 50 Call @ $1

This means the option contract is for 100 shares (the value 1 = 100 shares, or one option contract) of ABC stock. The option expires the third Friday in August. The strike price is $50, and the premium is $1. This is a low-risk strategy with your only risk limited to the premium, with high potential upside (thought the probability of going above the strike price may not be high). It's also low risk for the seller since they keep the premium and the worst case outcome is selling the shares at the strike price which was higher than the price of the shares at the time the contract was written, but lower than the market price at the time of sale.

For the buyer of this contract:

- The maximum loss is limited to the premium, which is the quoted price multiplied by 100 for the total number of shares, or $1 x 100 = $100.
- Maximum gain: Theoretically unlimited, depending on how much the share price exceeds the strike price.

Short or Naked Calls (role: seller)

We began our discussion with covered calls. In that case, as the seller of the option, the call was "covered" by the underlying stock. A *naked call* is one that is uncovered. That is, you write call options without owning the underlying stock. Remember for a call option, if you are forced into an assignment, you must sell the underlying shares. With a naked call, you face potential losses since you don't own the shares when you write the call. On the market, naked calls are known as "shorts". The ticker might look something like this:

Short 1 ABC Jun 25 Call @ $2

This tells us that the option contract expires the third Friday in June. The strike price is $25, and the premium is $2. In this case:

- The breakeven point is strike price + option premium = $25 + $2 = $27.
- Maximum gain is 100 shares x premium = $200.
- Maximum loss is unlimited, depending on how high the stock goes because you would have to buy the shares if assigned. Since this is high risk and you'd need the capital available to take care of the deal if the need arises, brokerages assign levels to options traders to determine whether or not they are allowed to participate in such high-risk trades. When you open an account to trade options, you'll need to know what your assigned level is to determine which types of trades you can make.

Short Puts (role: seller)

A short put, like a naked call, is a risky trading strategy and you'll be required to have capital available to risk. This is a small possible gain with a large possible loss option. Consider the following put:

Short 1 ABC Jul 30 Put @ $2

This option expires the third Friday in July, has a strike price of $30 and a premium of $2.

- Maximum gain: $2 premium x 100 shares = $200.
- Maximum loss: ($30 strike price - $2 premium) x 100 = $2,800.
- Break even: ($30 strike price - $2 premium) = $28.

Long Put (role: buyer)

For a long put, we're betting that the stock price is going to drop below the strike price. This is a lower risk strategy than a short put for the buyer. If the price fails to drop below the strike price, then you're only out the premium. Of course, to exercise your right to sell the shares, you'll have to have access to the capital necessary to buy them. We'll say our example is:

Long 1 ABC Sep 40 Put @ $3

The contract expires on the third Friday of September. The strike price is $40, and the premium is $3, so the cost to buy the contract is $3 x 100 = $300.

- Maximum loss: The maximum loss is the cost of the premium, so $3 x 100 = $300.
- Maximum gain: The maximum gain is given by (strike price – premium) x 100 = ($40 - $3) x 100 = $3,700.
- The breakeven point is strike price minus the premium, or $40 - $3 = $37.

So this is a lower risk strategy – since the maximum loss is much smaller than the potential gain.

For now, that is all we need to know about options. Our next step is to learn some of the basics of day trading.

Chapter 2: Day Trading – The Basics

Day trading means what it says. When you're day trading, you're going to buy and sell a stock within one day, and do so without waiting for close. A day trader is looking for stocks that have short term volatility. Of course, you're going to want to buy low and sell high. Although day traders are viewed by the general public as gamblers, this is far from reality. A day trader is using reasoned strategies to make profits. Of course, some day traders are better than others, they have more experience, they may study the markets better, and have a better sense of timing. However, things don't always go as planned, so day trading does carry a lot more risk than simply buying into stocks for the long term.

Of course, in the world of stocks, the word "long" has multiple meanings. When you buy a stock hoping that the price will go up, you're said to be buying long. Day traders, despite the very short-term nature of their buying and selling, are said to *buy long* because they are hoping for the price to go up. When you short a stock, you're hoping for the price to go down.

To take full advantage of the opportunities offered by being a day trader, you may need to have capital on account with your broker and possibly be approved for making certain transactions. Approval could depend on how much capital you can put up, and other things like maybe your creditworthiness. A brokerage is not going to take unnecessary risks. As we get into some of the strategies used by day traders, it will make more sense why this is the case. Keep in mind that these strategies are not exclusive to day traders, the only difference is that if you are day trading then you're going to carry them out to completion within one trading day.

Smart Money vs. Dumb Money

There are two general types of investors. The first is institutional investors. These are large investors like pension funds and hedge funds. Institutional investors are colloquially known as "smart money". They are called smart money because they have more information available and have tools at their disposal like Bloomberg terminals which cost a lot of money while giving them rapid information. Also controlling huge amounts of capital, they can even move the markets.

Retail investors are individual and small traders. This is the "dumb money" – in other words, that is you. Don't take offense, the term doesn't really mean that you are dumb in the sense of being stupid! Dumb money just means that relatively speaking, compared to the large institutional investors you don't have access to the same information at the same speed, so you're not going to be making trades that are as well-informed.

Selling short

Let's begin by looking at a strategy known as *selling short*. This strategy relies on being able to borrow shares from a broker so that you can profit on the share price decline. The process involves the following steps. First, you'll borrow shares from the broker. Then you sell them on the market. When the share price drops, then you'll buy the shares again, and then you return the shares to the broker.

Of course, this depends on things going in your favor. If the share price doesn't drop, you risk losing money.

To see how you could profit from this, we'll use a simple example. Let's say that ABC is trading at $20 a share at market opening. They're going to release a quarterly report and you're expecting bad news that will make the share price drop, at least for a while. You borrow 100 shares from the broker, and then you immediately sell them. So, you make:

$20 x 100 = $2,000

At this point, it's borrowed money since you must return the shares to the broker. If you're wrong and the price goes up, then you're going to have a loss. But let's say the news comes out and as you expected its very bad news. Say the share price drops to $14. Now you can buy 100 shares at this lower price:

$14 x 100 = $1,400

Then you immediately return the shares to the broker. So, you've made a profit given by:

Price you sold the borrowed shares – Price you paid to get them back = $2,000 - $1,400 = $600 profit.

Not bad eh? Who wouldn't want to make a quick $600 profit in an afternoon just sitting at their computer trading stocks?

Of course, it's not that easy. A lot of speculation goes into day trading, and you can bet wrong, as well as bet right. So maybe you bet wrong and lose $200 instead. Selling short requires that you closely study the stock market and the company you're going to short in order to avoid losses. Selling short may not be the best option for beginning day traders, since the risk that you'll end up owing money is high, even though the potential profits are large.

One or more trades

We've illustrated the process of selling short with a single trade. However, there are more options available. You can trade a given stock multiple times in a single day in the hopes of making profits.

Basic Strategies

Day traders rely on four basic strategies to make daily profits in the stock market. Let's review each of them.

Scalping

Chances are you're familiar with the concept of scalping tickets to an upcoming event, maybe a music concert or high demand sporting event. The idea is you buy the tickets at face value, then when it's sold out you show up at the venue and offer your tickets for sale at a premium price to make a profit.

Scaling isn't the same on the stock market, but scalping is the most basic strategy used by day traders. At its core is the notion of "buy low, sell high". When a day trader uses scalping, they buy the shares at a given price, and then sell immediately when they stand to make a profit. So, if you buy 100 shares of ABC company for $10 a share, a total investment of $10 x 100 = $1,000, you then closely monitor the share price to sell when it becomes profitable. Suppose that at first, it drops to $9.50 a share, and bounces around a bit. Then it jumps up to $11.75 a share. At this point you'll sell right away, earning:

100 shares x $11.75/share = $1,175

Since you invested $1,000 to buy the shares, you've made a quick profit of $175. Scalping is a good way to get your feet wet with day trading, it's a very basic strategy. Of course, you're not going to get into scalping on a random basis, you're going to want to study the markets, keeping up with financial news, and choosing companies that are likely to show an increase in share price that day. This illustrates that day trading is not something you can do while at work or while going out to play golf. You must take an active role in the markets in order to make it work on a systematic basis. Sure, you could buy some stock before heading to the office, and maybe you get lucky and check at lunch and the price is higher so you can sell at a profit. But often, the price may have gone up into a profitable range and may have either dropped down so your profit is a lot less than what it could have been or you're even in a losing position. Scalping isn't very complicated, but it does require that you stay on top of the markets to increase your odds of success and to maximize your success if it does arrive.

Scalping is a pretty basic concept, and that isn't really day trading (although you can certainly do it). Day trading involves planning ahead using well thought out strategies. The first strategy that we'll look at involves using *pivot points*.

Daily Pivot

The stock market is very volatile, in some sense being guided by chaotic randomness as prices rise and fall at the whims of large numbers of buyers and sellers. Of course, the volatility isn't entirely random, and over the long-term, it gets smoothed out. However, the day trader attempts to take short term advantage of that volatility.

Daily pivot is a strategy that centers on buying your shares at the low point of the day and then (hopefully) selling them at the high point of the day. This strategy does involve a bit of guesswork, there is really no way to know with any certainty what the low and high points of the day are going to be ahead of time – so there is a strong possibility that you will guess wrong.

Of course, we don't want to trade based on a "guess", we're going to use a strategy based on facts (it still may be right or wrong, but we rely on real data to make our trading decisions). This idea is based on the fact that most of the time when dealing with short term movements of stocks, trading is going to proceed based in some part on what the shares have done in the very recent past.

So you calculate what's called a pivot point. This has three inputs: the previous day's high, low, and close. The pivot point is simply the average of the thee:

Pivot point = (high + low + close)/3

Now suppose that we have stock for XYZ. The high, low, and close the previous day were $102, $97, and $100. The pivot point is then:

Pivot point = ($102 + $97 + $100)/3 = $99.67

Now to figure out how to proceed with our trades the following day, we will calculate some *support* points and points. We will explain what the means in a moment, but first let's learn how to calculate the support points.

Support point 1 = (pivot point x 2) – high from the previous day

Support point 2 = Pivot point – (high – low)

Our support points in this case would be:

S1 = ($99.67 x 2) - $102 = $97.33

S2 = ($99.67) – (102 - $97) = $94.67

Next, we need two resistance points. The formulas used for these are:

R1 = (pivot point x 2) – low from previous day

R2 = Pivot Point + (high – low)

For our example the resistance points are:

R1 = ($99.67 x 2) - $97 = $102.34

$$R2 = \$99.67 + (\$102 - \$97) = \$104.67$$

We see that the resistance points are above the pivot point, with R1 being a little bit above, and R2 being the most above the pivot point. The support points are below the pivot point, with S1 being a little bit below, and S2 being the lowest point. The numbers R1, R2, S1, S2, and P are only valid for one trading day. Each trading day you need to calculate them using the previous days trading data, prior to the stock market open. You can find pivot point trading calculators on Google.

Stop loss points

A stop loss is a point that is chosen as a kind of insurance to limit losses incurred on security. This is done with a stop-loss order. What you do is you place an order with the broker to buy or sell the stock when it reaches a certain price. As an example, suppose you buy XYZ stock at $100. After you purchase the shares, you can place a stop-loss order for $95. What this does is your shares will be sold if the price drops to $95.

That protects you from incurring even more losses if the stock is tanking.

The buy signal

The point of doing these calculations is to determine when to buy, when to sell, and when to cut your losses. The buy signal occurs when the price of the stock goes above the pivot point with *conviction*. You are bullish on the stock, expecting the price to keep rising (it may not). Your first profit target is given by R1.

By conviction, that means that the stock price is moving up fast. The volume also figures in when evaluating conviction, more volume means more conviction. If there are a lot of volumes and the price is moving up fast, that means more buyers are bullish on the stock.

For our case, the pivot point was $99.67. If the price breaks strongly above this, we take that as a buy signal. The previous days close was $100 so we will say for this example that the share price jumped to $101. We could decide to buy the shares at this price.

The profit point is R1, which is $102.34 based on our calculations. You could choose to sell if the stock price hits R1. However, if the stock is rising rapidly, then you can choose R2 as your profit target. In that case, you would wait until the price hits $104.67 to sell.

If you are right, then you purchased shares of XYZ stock at $101 per share. If we buy 100 shares, then we are in for:

100 x $101 = $10,100

Now suppose that it does hit R2. We immediately sell, so our gross revenue is:

100 x $104.67 = $10,467

We've made a profit of $10,467 - $10,100 = $367. If that was the only trade, we made that day, then we've made a pretty nice daily income of $367.

Of course, things don't always go as planned, which is why you need a stop loss point. You do this so that you can minimize losses and avoid losing your shirt. Whether you stick to R1 or R2 as the point at which you'll sell for a profit or not will depend on how rapidly the stock is going up. So, you'll be looking at a measure of its momentum. The stop loss points S1 and S2 correspond to each case. For R1, which is $102.34, your stop loss point would be S1 = $97.33. If the stock is shooting up and immediately goes above R1, you can take P as your stop loss. If it has gone up to R1 but doesn't show more conviction (i.e. that it's going to go up to R2) then you sell at about R1 and take the smaller profits.

If you are shorting a stock as described in the previous section, then the roles of the Rx and Sx points reverse, with R1 & R2 playing the role of stop loss points and S1 and S2 representing profits.

When to use pivot points

There is no solid agreement on this. Some traders believe that pivot points are at their highest accuracy right after the market opens, and so they believe you should utilize them within the first hour of trading. Others believe that the first half-hour of the trading day will have too much volatility, so you should wait before using them.

Morning or Opening Gaps

A morning gap is when a stock opens higher or lower than it closed the previous day. Suppose that XYZ stock closed at $50. If it opens the next morning it opens at $51, then this would be a $1 gap up. On the other hand, if the stock opened at $49.50, that would be a 50-cent gap down.

A strategy that day traders use is called *fade the gap*. There are two options:

- If the stock opens up, take a short position.
- If the stock opens down, take a long position.

The bet while using this strategy is that the stock is going to return to a value near the previous days close. This is called *filling the gap*. In other words, you're betting on the opposite trend the stock had at the opening of the markets.

With options trading:

- If the stock opens up, you'll buy puts on the stock.
- If the stock opens down, you'll buy calls on the stock.

Here is an example. On April 18, 2019, Apple closed at $203.86 a share. The markets were closed on Friday for Easter, on Monday, April 22, 2019, Apple opened at $202.65 a share.

204.53 USD +0.67 (0.33%) ↑
Closed: Apr 22, 4:32 PM EDT · Disclaimer
After hours 204.53 0.00 (0.00%)

| 1 day | 5 days | 1 month | 6 months | YTD | 1 year | 5 years | Max |

202.65 USD Mon, Apr 22 9:30 AM

206
204
202
200
198

Apr 16   Apr 17   Apr 18   Apr 22

Since the stock opened lower than the previous day's close, you'd take a long position on the stock, hoping that it would close the gap and rise back up to the closing price. You could buy stock and hold it until it (hopefully) rose to a profitable point, or you could buy call options on the stock. Looking at what the stock did, we see that had we bought call options on Apple at the beginning of the trading day, this would have been successful speculation. By 4 PM the stock had closed at $204.53 a share. But as a day trader, you would have closed your position using this technique when it had gotten back to the previous days close.

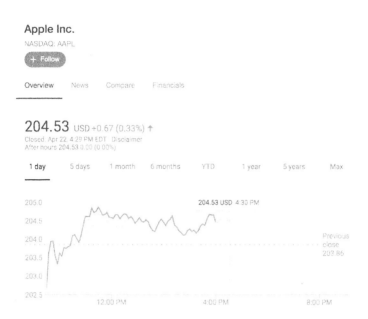

Apple Inc.
NASDAQ: AAPL

+ Follow

Overview   News   Compare   Financials

204.53 USD +0.67 (0.33%) ↑
Closed: Apr 22, 4:29 PM EDT · Disclaimer
After hours 204.53 0.00 (0.00%)

1 day   5 days   1 month   6 months   YTD   1 year   5 years   Max

This was a fortuitous example since the stock happened to go significantly above the previous close and stayed up most of the day. Of course, this is a risky venture, since that is not always going to be something that works out.

However, the data indicate that is actually a fairly reasonable approach. Most stocks to fill the gap at some point during the following trading day. It's estimated that 68% of stocks will completely fill the gap, and 78% will fill the gap at least half-way. You're making a decent bet that will be right most of the time. There is some risk in that if you're waiting for it to fill the gap completely and it's at the half-way point, that it doesn't get to where you're hoping it will go and end up trading without maximizing potential profits.

When the morning gap is down, the odds of success are better. In other words, it's more likely that a stock that opens down is going to increase in price during the trading day rather than a stock opening up and decreasing in price. So, calls are better buying options than puts if you are using this technique, but of course, you will have to look at the specific stock that you're looking to use for this technique. Each individual case will vary depending on what is going on with the specific stock in question.

Opening Range Breakouts
Another day trading strategy is opening range breakouts. The *opening range* is the first half-hour of

the trading day. For the opening range, you mark down the low of the first half-hour and the high of the first half-hour. Suppose that XYZ opens at $90, and then the low of the first half-hour is $89, and the high of the first half-hour is $91. Then the opening range is the difference, or $2. What you'll be looking for is for a breakout, meaning that the stock price either rises with conviction above the high point of the opening range or drops below the low point of the opening range.

If the stock begins to go above the high of the opening range with conviction you can buy the stock, in anticipation that it will continue to increase the rest of the day or most of the rest of the day.

Fading

Fading is a bet against dumb money in the stock market. The technique is based on shorting stocks that have moved upward rapidly, typically in the first hour after market open. The idea is based on the belief that the stock is overbought, that is retail investors have jumped in on stock and bid up to the price based on some news about the stock. During the process, eager retail investors will bid the price up beyond its intrinsic value, so as the trading day goes on the price will begin dropping.

The point to get in and short the stock is to look for when the upswing begins slowing down or fading. Obviously, fading is a high-risk strategy, you don't have the same information available as the institutional investors so may be guessing wrong even when it appears that the rise of the stock is sputtering. You should always protect yourself with a stop-loss.

Candlesticks

A candlestick is a marking on a stock chart or graph that represents the following four data points:

- Open
- High
- Low

- Close

Candlesticks are colored red or green on a chart. Just for the sake of seeing a representation, here is a screenshot of a couple of candlesticks for a specific stock:

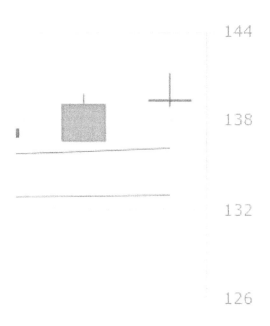

Candlesticks can be green or red in color. The rectangle shown on the chart is the body of the candlestick. If the candlestick is green, the bottom represents the opening price, and the top represents the closing price. The narrow lines emanating from the candlestick body are called the wicks. If the candlestick is green color, that means the price of the stock went up over the given time period. If you have a monthly chart, then the green color indicates that by the close of the day, for that day the stock went up in price.

A red candlestick indicates that the price of the stock went up for the period of measurement. If the time period is one month, then the top indicates the opening price, while the bottom of the body indicates the opening price.

Different time periods can be illustrated on a graph. In many cases, we are interested in short term price changes for day trading. We can look at a chart that shows whether the price went up or down over a five-minute period. If the price went up over the five-minute periods, the candlestick is green in color. The top of the candlestick body indicates the price at the end of the five-minute period. The bottom indicates the price at the start of the five-minute period.

On the other hand, if the candlestick is colored red, over the given five-minute period, the top represents the price at the start of the five minute period, while the bottom of the body represents the price at the end of the vie minute period.

Let's illustrate this with pictures. Here is the candlestick when it is red in color on the chart:

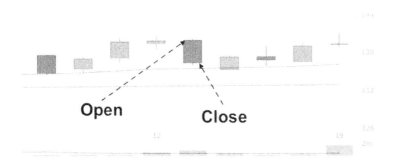

For a green candlestick, the chart representation is the opposite:

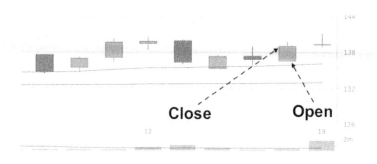

While the top and bottom of the body represent the open and close, the wicks are used to represent the high price, and the low price, respectively.

The top of the candlestick wick represents the high stock price for the day. The bottom of the wick represents the low price of the stock for the day. Or, if the time period is for one day, the ranges represent the change in price over five-minute intervals. So close is the price of the stock at the end of the five-minute period, while open is the price of the stock at the beginning of the five minute period.

Most often, when it comes to day trading, you're going to be looking at trading intervals for one single day so the prices represented will tell you how the stock moved over five-minute intervals:

- The high price of the stock over the five-minute interval.
- The low price of the stock over the five-minute interval.
- The closing or end price at the end of the five-minute interval.
- The opening or starting price of the stock over the five-minute interval.

When looking at candlestick charts, you're interested in knowing whether a bearish or bullish engulfing pattern presents itself. So, you pick a candlestick somewhere in the chart and compare that candlestick to the one to the left of the selected candlestick.

- If the candlestick on the right side is red and it engulfs or covers the entire range of the candlestick immediately to the left which is green (that is, the trading period five minutes prior), that is a bearish candlestick pattern. Remember that green means the price of the stock went up over the period. If the price goes down over the subsequent period (indicated by red color), then this is a bearish candlestick. If this occurs at the top of an uptrend, then this is considered a reversal candle.

- A bullish engulfing or candlestick pattern occurs when you see a red candlestick pattern followed by a green candlestick pattern which engulfs or encompasses the previous candlestick. If a red candlestick is followed by a larger green candlestick at the bottom of a downtrend, then this is considered to be an indication of a reversal.

Here, we have red followed by green at the bottom of a downturn. The green candlestick to the right, which completely covers the red candlestick to the left, is said to engulf the red candlestick. If you are long, this is a good sign. This indicates a reversal, so the stock price can be expected to increase.

On the other hand, suppose we have a red candle that engulfs a green candle. The red is to the right:

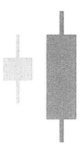

If you are shorting a stock, this is a good sign. Otherwise, it's a bad sign. This indicates a reversal if you are at the top of an upturn. That is, the larger red candle which engulfs the green candle to the left (i.e.

earlier in time) indicates that the stock is in reversal, which means that the stock is heading to a downturn. If you are long on the stock, it's a bad sign. If you are shorting the stock, or invested in puts, that means that it's a good sign, i.e. that the stock can be expected to be heading into a downturn.

- If you see several red candles heading down in a downturn, and then you see a green candle that engulfs the previous red candle, this is bullish – so may indicate a coming upturn on the stock price. So if you are bullish on the stock, this indicates a buying opportunity if you are long, or if you want to buy calls.
- If you see several green candles going up, and then there is a red candle the engulfs the previous (to the left) green candle, then this is bearish, that is we expect a downturn in the stock price. If you are buying puts, this is the time to buy.

These are guidelines, but not rules. So, while it might be accurate, it's not going to be accurate all the time.

A shooting star or "inverted hammer" is a candlestick with the top wick much longer than the bottom wick.

The body is small, meaning that the opening and closing price for the time period is not much different. The long wick indicates that the price went up a lot over the period and then closed close to the opening price. A shooting star at the top of an uptrend is considered bearish. It indicates a coming downtrend, which would be bearish if you are long, but good if you want to buy puts.

If this occurs at the bottom of a downtrend, it's an inverted hammer. That is bullish, indicating the stock price should be going up.

These are reversal candles, so are important to recognize in charts. In the chart below, notice that the candle has little or no wick below it, and it has a small body with a long wick above. The candle is red in color. This indicates that it is a bearish candle. This is a sell signal if you are long in the stock, or if you are looking to short, that is a buy signal.

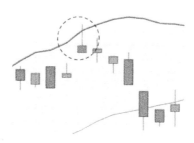

Chapter 3: More Trading Strategies

In this chapter, we will continue our look at commonly used day trading strategies. We will begin by looking at what is known as ABCD patterns, bull flags, reversals, moving averages, support, and resistance, and then finally Bollinger bands.

ABCD

The ABCD strategy is a basic strategy that looks for a certain pattern in stock to get an idea of what the trend is in the market. What you are looking for is a stock that starts low and rises to a high point A, and then drops back down to a low point B. Point A represents the breakout level, that is if the stock passes point A, a second time during the trading day you're expecting it to rise significantly, representing an opportunity where you can sell for profit. So why would point A drop down? This is a point when many investors have decided to sell because they are happy with their profits and they are leery of the stock continues to increase.

As the stock begins to be sold off, at some point it will reach a low point, which will be point B in the chart. The low point occurs when new buyers overtake sellers that began selling as a result of the stock reaching the high point A. Then, when more buyers come in the stock will settle on a new low point, C, which will be higher than point B. If this pattern is established, you take your risk level as point B. After it hits point C, it may begin moving upward again. This is a signal of a good buying opportunity so we may jump in at this point. If the ABCD pattern is realized, it will move up to a new high point D, where we can sell and take our profits.

In the chart below, if the stock goes above point A, this is considered breakout. Time to consider selling. This is a bearish ABCD, which means you see a time to sell and take profits before the stock drops again. Point B could you're your stop-loss point. This is a bearish ABCD, meaning we expect it to drop.

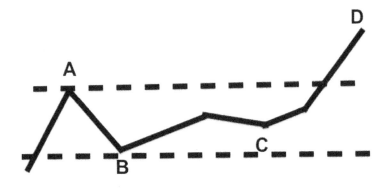

Example- suppose that XYZ Stock opens strongly, going from $50 a share up to $60 a share. Then over the next hour, it drops to $40 a share. It then rises up to $55 a share and drops a little bit to $53 a share. At this point, we will consider buying. Our risk level is the lowest point which was $40 a share. If the stock starts turning upward, we buy. So, we can take any point between that and our purchase point as a stop-loss, so, for example, we could set a stop loss at $45. It then continues upward to point D, say in this case it rises to

$63 a share, where we sell to take our profits before the stock drops again.

We can also have a bullish ABCD pattern. This is where the stock looks to rise.

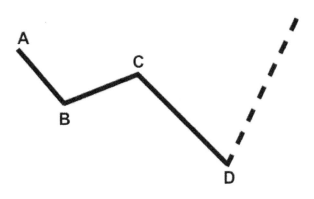

In this case, we buy at point D. This can be done buying calls or actually going long on the stock.

When we see ABCD patterns, the lines AB and CD are known as the legs. The line BC is either called the correction or the retracement. A retracement is a temporary reversal of the stock price. In that case, the stock has an overall upward trend for the day. So, the retracement is seen as a temporary downturn that is going to reverse. A correction is a downturn of 10% or more in the price of the stock. A correction is an ideal time to buy a stock because odds are it's going to go back up and possibly strongly so. In the second chart, at point D there has been a correction. In the first ABCD graph, we see a retracement, on the way to an overall upward trend.

Ideally, the lines AB and CD should be of equal length.

The Bull Flag

A bull flag is a strong upward trend in the stock. However, after shooting upward, the stock enters a phase of consolidation, when people slow down or stop buying, but before a new rise may begin. The "flag pole" is a steep rise in the price of the stock over a very short time period. The "flag" is a time period when the price is high but stays about the same. A bull flag is a symbol of a buying opportunity for a stock that has already shown a significant increase. You should set your desired profit, buy and then sell when it begins increasing again up to the point where you have set to take your profit. You should always include a stop-loss, a bull flag is no guarantee and the price might actually start dropping.

When there is a bull flag, it is bordered along the bottom by a level below which the stock is not dropping, known as the support. On the top, there is a level above which the stock is not rising. This is called *resistance*. Eventually, the stock is going to break out of the resistance so you want to buy before this happens, as the stock may see a rapid rise again. A bull flag may occur multiple times during the day as the stock trends upward.

The Bear Flag

A bear flag is equivalent to a bull flag but when a stock is tanking, so it represents opportunities to short the stock or buy puts. In this case, the stock will drop by a large amount over a short time period. It's going to have an upside down flag pole, and then a flag at the bottom where the stock stays within a narrow range for a while, bounded by resistance and support. This is a buying opportunity if you are looking to short the stock so you can buy a put with an appropriate strike price. The hope here is that the stock will continue it's a downward trend when it breaks out of the flag. It may do so rapidly and then hit another flag later in the trading day.

Reversals

A reversal is a major change in the direction of the price of the stock. So, the trend completely shifts and moves in the opposite direction. In order to look for reversals, look at the candlesticks on a stock market chart. The body of the candlesticks and its size relative to the previous (to the left) candlesticks is what is important. First, let's consider a signal for a reversal where a declining stock price is going to be going up in the future. If the candlestick of the most recent time is larger and fully engulfs or covers the candlestick to the left, and it's the opposite color, i.e. a green candlestick following red candlesticks, this indicates a reversal of a downtrend into an increasing stock price. This is a good time to go long or buy calls.

On the other hand, let's now consider the case where the stock price is going up, with multiple green candlesticks in a row. Then it is followed by an engulfing red candlestick. This indicates a reversal so we will expect the stock price to begin going down. That is, this is a point where we should short the stock, or if trading options invest in puts.

The larger the engulfing candlestick, the stronger the reversal signal is. That indicates that the change in direction has a significant conviction behind the reversal, which is the confidence of investors, larger volume and the price will change in larger amounts over short time periods. If the wicks engulf the wicks of the previous period, that is an even stronger signal that a reversal is underway.

When using reversals as a trading strategy, you need a minimum of five candlesticks in a five-minute chart.

Then look at the relative strength index, which helps you evaluate overbought or oversold stocks. The RSI ranges from 0-100. At the top of an uptrend, if the RSI is above 90 that indicates that the stock is overbought and is probably going to be heading into a downturn. On the other hand, if you are looking at the bottom of a downturn, if the RSI is 10 or below, this indicates that the stock is oversold. That could be a signal that is about to see a price increase.

When looking for reversals, indecision candlesticks can be important in combination with the other variables discussed here. An indecision candlestick indicates neither an upturn or a downturn. That is if you see a downturn followed by several indecision candlesticks, that could mean that the stock is about to turn upward again. Or vice versa – if an upturn is followed by several indecision candlesticks, that can indicate a reversal resulting in a downward trending stock price.

Looking at the wicks can be important as well. When the lower wick of the candlestick is longer, that may indicate that the price dropped over the period of the candlestick, but the stock turned and was bought up. On the other hand, if the candlestick has a long wick at the top, that may indicate that the stock was bid up too much over the period. Traders lost interest and began selling off the stock.

At any time there appears to be a reversal, a trend of indecision candles or stagnation represents a buying opportunity no matter which direction the stock may be trending. That is if you are in the midst of a downturn and the stock is moving sideways, then it may be a good time to go long on it or buy calls. The opposite is true if the stock is at the top of a potential reversal. If it's moving sideways, it may be a good time to invest in puts. Keep in mind that this does not always work. The best indicator is whether or not a green (red) candlestick following a red (green) candlestick which engulfs the candlestick to the left is the best indicator of a coming reversal.

Moving Average

Another trading strategy that can be exploited is the moving average. This may help when a trader is looking for entry and exit points while trading. First, we will look at the simple moving average crossover strategy. Look at candlestick charts when considering moving averages with a two-minute interval.

You can include multiple moving averages in a chart with different periods. A faster-moving average on a chart is colored red and a slower moving average is colored green. A buy signal is a red line moving above the green line. That is, it breaks above the green line. A sell signal is when the green line is above the red line. If the lines are overlapping, then that means to wait. So, to profit, when the faster moving average tops the slower moving average, you go long, which means buy the stock or buy a call option. Then when the red line (or faster-moving average) goes below the slower moving average that is a sell signal. If you went long you sell your stock. It could also be an indication to buy puts.

A stop loss should be five or ten percent below the moving average line.

Solid profits can be realized when the stock breaks out high above the moving average. You can choose to take a half-position at this point, in order to lower your risk.

Following the moving average leaves your investments exposed to the markets for a longer period of time. If you are a beginner to day trading, this can increase your risk. For that reason, many beginners avoid following the moving average. It will be necessary if looking at moving averages to stay exposed to the market for several hours. On the other hand, some beginners will prefer this method, because you have more time to make decisions regarding your trades. One of the things that you will need to learn when day trading is that you have to think fast on your feet. If that is something that causes you an issue, using moving averages can help you get more attuned to the markets while utilizing a slower method. Large gaps in entry and exit points can also be an advantage, helping you get a nice profit on your trades that helps wipe out the commission fees.

Bollinger Bands

Bollinger bands are a very popular indicator for day traders, looking for price actions and indicators for strengthening or weakening. These were developed by none other than John Bollinger. Bollinger bands are adaptive trading bands. A trading band is simply a range of prices for security (aka stock). In particular, Bollinger bands represent:

- Volatility
- The extent of price movement
- They indicate trend lines defining support and resistance

Bollinger bands are calculated using standard deviation. However, you don't need to be an expert in statistics to understand how Bollinger bands are calculated or what they represent. In short, a Bollinger band is calculated relative to some average of prices, for example, the moving average over a given number of periods. What the Bollinger band represents then, is the spread of prices about that average.

Bollinger bands only measure closing prices and how to spread out they are. Typically, they measure the 20 periods moving average, but they can be used for 50 or 100 periods.

Bollinger bands are dynamic. You will see them around the candlesticks in a stock chart. When they narrow, that is known as a volatility squeeze. If they spread out, that is a volatility spread.

- If the bands are narrow, that indicates that the prices over that period are falling within a smaller range (i.e. the closing prices for each period are relatively similar to each other).
- If the bands are wider, that indicates a greater spread in prices, that is individual prices differ

from each other a lot more – put another way, there is more volatility.

What signals are there with Bollinger bands that a day trader can look for?

- If wick of a candlestick at the bottom hits the Bollinger band, that can be taken as a buy signal. The stock is oversold, so it's a good time to buy.
- When the candlestick touches or crosses the upper Bollinger band, then the stock is overbought. Time to sell.

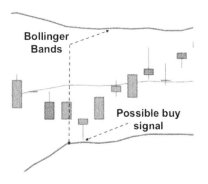

Sell signals, overbought

Of course, the vice versa applies, if a candle hits the top band, it may not be a sell signal, you may want to short or buy puts.

When the candlesticks are hitting the Bollinger bands, this may indicate a reversal. A hammer at the bottom of a reversal touching the bottom Bollinger band is a nice buy signal in many cases. Reversal candlesticks that touch a Bollinger band are a solid indicator that there is really a reversal coming.

In the opposite direction, if you are looking to short a stock or invest in puts, then you want to look for shooting stars that touch the upper Bollinger band.

This can indicate a reversal or a coming downturn. If you are long on a stock and this condition arises, that indicates that it is a good time to sell.

When using Bollinger bands, you will want to look at the shape of the candlestick itself. This can strengthen or weaken your indicators. If you see a hammer at the bottom of the Bollinger bands, this can indicate a coming upturn in the stock so it's a good time to go long. On the other hand, if you see a shooting star touching the top Bollinger band, that may be an indicator that it is either a good time to sell or a good time to short or buy puts. Using Bollinger bands is not going to be a perfect indicator, but you can combine your observations about the shapes of the candlesticks and whether or not they are shooting stars or hammers together with the Bollinger bands to get a reasonable conjecture as to whether the stock is likely to move in one direction or in the opposite direction. In other words, looking at the candlesticks together with their relationship to the Bollinger bands will help you determine whether or not a given stock is primed to reverse.

Support and Resistance

We have touched on support and resistance earlier, here we will discuss the definitions in more detail. Support and resistance refer to lines on a pricing chart that act as barriers. That is, a support line will be found at the bottom of the chart that indicates a pricing level that serves as a minimum. Put another way, it is not expected that the price of the security in question will drop below the support. Looking toward increasing or higher prices, the resistance line is a top or maximum limit to expected changes in price. That is, it is not expected that the price of a security will go above the resistance line.

Support and resistance levels are primarily used to identify points at which the probabilities support a reversal, pause, or prevailing trend in the stock price. Since support is found at the bottom of a pricing chart, this means that the support represents a point where a downward trend can be expected to pause, and possibly reverse. On the other hand, the resistance is at the top of a stock pricing chart, hence it represents a point where an upward trend can be expected to pause, and possibly reverse and so turn into a downward trend. Of course, not all pauses result in reversals so you will have to look toward other signals such as the candlesticks and the Bollinger bands.

Trends in market activity are set by the basic economic principles of supply and demand. If the price of a security is dropping rapidly, the lower it drops the more demand for the stock is going to be generated. The support line represents the point at which demand is expected to overtake the selloff and possibly send the price of the stock upward again.

The resistance line works in converse fashion. As the price of a stock rises, at some point demand begins to slip. A sell-off begins which leads to declining prices.

A zone of support defines an entry point. That is, in simple language, this is a good point at which to buy the stock (go long or buy calls). This view, of course, may be in error. It's entirely possible that the stock can violate the price level and continue its decline until it hits new support, and a new entry point is defined.

Now let's consider a zone of resistance. This is where the stock price has been increasing. A zone of resistance defines a possible exit point. That is, it is expected (but not certain) that the stock is peaking out and this is a good time to get out. So if you are in a long position, in a zone of resistance you may want to sell. Once again, it is possible that the stock will violate the price level, and the zone of resistance may be an illusion as the stock begins to go up again until it reaches a new zone of resistance.

Traders act on the belief that a zone of support or resistance will not be broken. Of course, in many cases their bet is wrong. In that case, you can close and take a small loss. It's important to avoid letting emotions get the best of you in these situations. If you let emotion take over, you may hold onto your position too long hoping that somehow it can or will reverse course. Taking this approach can lead to larger losses. It's best to get out when you see the first signal that you've made an error.

So how do you spot a zone of resistance? Simply put, it's a price at which the stock approaches multiple times but can't seem to get past. You can define a zone of resistance over any time period you like, you could be talking about over an hour in the case of day trading or over the course of weeks or months for regular stock trading. If we take a hypothetical example, for XYZ stock it may see peaks at $98, $99.75, $99.50 and $99.85 over the course of a few hours. Then we may define the zone of resistance for that day at $100. A trader may decide to either short the stock, invest in puts, or if they are long, they may sell and close their position.

A zone of support works in the same way. There is a bottoming out price that the stock seems to keep approaching but doesn't cross and go lower. In that case, the trader may see this stock as a buying opportunity, it's a stock that is soon to rise in price. For the hypothetical XYZ stock, we could envision the zone of support being something like $90.

Trending is important when looking at support and resistance levels. It's not going to be very long that a stock is trapped in some zone where the level of support and resistance remains the same. It's going to be trending over time. With the changes in price, the support and resistance levels can change. For our hypothetical XYZ stock, if the company is healthy and growing, then we can imagine that it will eventually break the $100 barrier and climb up to a new level, say where the zone of resistance is $108, and the zone of support is $100. Depending on how volatile the stock is at a given moment, it could make this move quickly – within one single day.

It's useful to pay attention to moving averages when thinking about zones of support and resistance. When the moving average is below the actual price lines of the stock (that is the stock is trading at prices above the moving average), then that indicates a new zone of support. Conversely, when the stock is trading below the moving average, we have found a zone of resistance. Moving averages can also be used to look at the timing of when to enter and exit trades. If the price drops below the moving average, this indicates an exit point.

Risk

Formally defined, the risk is the difference between the entry price and the stop loss price. Suppose that stock XYZ is trading at $40. If you buy 100 shares of XYZ and then put in a stop-loss order of $35 a share, your risk is simply given by:

Risk = $40 - $35 = $5

Your *position size* is simply the number of shares that are bought in a given transaction.

Chapter 4: 10 Tips for Successful Day Trading

Day trading is a double-edged sword, you can reap substantial rewards, but you could lose your shirt by betting wrong. But it doesn't have to be an activity that carries huge amounts of risk. By following a few commonsense tips, you can minimize your risks and ensure that your profits are more likely.

Set Aside Capital for Day Trading

Don't be the person that bets the farm on hoping to cash in big. You should set aside capital that you are willing to lose for day trading. More importantly, you should set aside an amount of capital that you can afford to lose so that you're not begging relatives for money to pay your rent if your trades go bad.

Use Stop Losses

Even the most careful day trader can run into trouble. You can minimize your losses by planning ahead of time. Each time you place an order, make sure to use stop losses so that if your bet turns out to be wrong, your losses will be minimized.

Do your homework

As they say, knowledge is power. People who fail as day traders are people that buy and sell stocks based on superficial looks at the markets and relying on hunches. Those who make long term profits are those who carefully study the markets. That means being familiar with the stock market, recent behavior on the stock market, the companies you're looking to trade and the economy at large. Day trading is going to be a full-time activity. You will need to keep up with the economic outlook in the short term. You'll need to know what the Fed is going to be doing with interest rates. You'll have to follow international trade and look for political events that can impact the markets. You will need to read financial websites daily and subscribe to publications like the Wall Street Journal, Bloomberg and the Financial Times. You'll also need to spend time watching CNBC and Fox Business to get the latest news as soon as possible. It's also a good idea to make short lists of companies so that you can study several in detail so that you are acting on good information rather than playing guessing games.

Start Small

When you are learning how to day trade, chances are you're going to have a lot of failures. Therefore, it's best to start with small trades with small amounts of capital and limited numbers of shares. Buying options is a good way to start as well since you can speculate only risking the premiums rather than spending large amounts of money upfront. When you start small you can gain the necessary experience without losing all your capital first. As you gain experience and confidence you can increase the amount invested.

No Penny Stocks

Stick with stocks on the major stock exchange. Now and then, penny stocks will turn out to be hidden gems, but most of the time there is a reason that they are penny stocks. They are best avoided as they'll be losers most of the time.

Time for Volatility

The first and last hours of the trading day are when a lot of people will be making their moves for the day, either bidding stocks up or frantically selling. The mid-day is going to be a time of lower volatility. When you are first starting out, you might want to avoid the first half-hour of trading.

Practice Makes Perfect

Consider doing practice trades for a while. That is study the techniques used in day trading and then look at real data in the markets to decide what strategies you'd employ with a given stock, and then follow it without actually making the trade. The point here is to practice without risking capital for a short time period so that you can gain some experience before actually trading. There are stock trading simulators you can play with, for example:

https://ninjatrader.com

https://tradingsim.com

Don't get greedy

Using pivot points is a good strategy. It's going to be tempting to try and wait things out when a stock is moving rapidly in the direction you're betting on. But if you wait too long to act, you may end up missing out on profits. Don't get greedy and take what profits you can get using pre-determined limits.

Avoid Being Taken Over by Emotion

This is related to the last point, but it also relates to panic. If you're long on security but it doesn't look good for a while, don't panic and get out too early. This is the converse of being too greedy. It's human nature to panic, but in the stock markets, that's what the amateurs do. Using the pivot point example, you know ahead of time what your limits are. Using limit orders is the best way to avoid panic because you'll have your exit strategy set up already, so it will happen automatically.

Plan your trade and trade your plan

The key to succeeding while day trading is to plan ahead. You should already have your strategy mapped out before you move on it. You will have to act fast when the buying or selling condition arrives, but you won't need to think about it or agonize with emotion if you're planned things out ahead of time.

Chapter 5: Getting Started with Day Trading

The first thing to consider when getting started in day trading, is which market that you want to use in order to trade. That may sound like an odd question to consider at this point, but depending on how much capital you have, choosing the right market is critical. The important thing to recognize with day trading is that day traders routinely have strings of losses. And we are not talking about amateurs here, experienced day traders will experience losses on a routine basis. Of course, you expect that over time you are going to make profits, but just like flipping a penny can result in 5 tails in a row, making many day trades can result in many losses before a big win hit. So, if you're trading a significant amount of your capital, a string of losses could leave you going broke very quickly. Thousands of dollars can be at stake in an individual trade. For these reasons, there are some rules and recommendations in place to help you avoid getting into super big trouble, but the rules may make day trading seem less appealing especially if you cannot come up with the required capital.

Things to consider before getting started

Day trading isn't a hobby or a game. It's a serious business, and just like any serious business day trading is going to require a serious commitment even before you get started.

- Day trading requires a serious time commitment. You are going to have to study the financial markets, keep up with financial news, and spend time at your computer pouring over financial data. Do you have the time to do all of these things? It's basically a full-time job. You're not going to be a day trader while working your 9-5 and expect to be successful. The day traders who are successful are 100% committed.
- Are you willing to practice before actually beginning day trading? Jumping in and risking

tens of thousands of dollars without experience is a bad idea. We have listed links to practice software that lets you simulate stock market trading. Are you willing to spend several months honing your skills using practice methods before actually day trading with real money? You can even open "demo" accounts with many brokers. Consider working on this and practicing now, and then getting into real investing when you've honed your skills.

- Do you have adequate capital to get started? The U.S. government has a $25,000 minimum capital requirement to begin day trading. Do you have the money already? And is this actual money you can lose without getting into serious financial trouble?

Choose a broker

If you are already investing in stocks independently (that is outside an employer or a mutual fund) you may already have a broker that can also act as a broker for day trading purposes. Top brokers that retail investors can use include Ally Bank, TD Ameritrade, Trade Station, Interactive Brokers, ETrade, Charles Schwab, and many others.

Trading on the Stock Market

Of course, you can buy as few or as many shares of stock as you like, but experts advise that you need to have at least $25,000 in the capital that you can risk day trading in order to trade on the stock market. Making four trades in a week will qualify as being a day trader. If you plan to day trade four days per week, it's recommended that you have $30,000, in order to give yourself a bit of a buffer over the minimum. However, this value is quoted on the assumption that you're going to be trading actual shares of stock. It is recommended that your maximum risk on trade be limited to 1% of your total capital.

It's important to know your risk and position risk. Position risk is the number of shares times the risk. If you buy a stock at $20, and the stop-loss is $19, then your risk is $1. If you buy 500 shares, then your position risk is:

500 x ($20-$19) = $500

Stocks with higher volatility will require more risk than stocks with lower volatility. A day trader of stock can access leverage, typically at a rate of 4:1, allowing them to access more shares of stock than they could afford with their own capital.

A good way to get in on day trading on the stock market is --- you guessed it – by trading options. Buying an options contract only requires that you invest in the premium. Trading in options lets you leverage your money.

Futures Markets

You can day trade on futures markets with less capital. This can still let you get involved with stocks, however. For example, you can day trade the S&P 500 on the futures markets with a fraction of the capital required for day trading stocks. You can probably get started on this for between $1,000-$2,500. The daily range of futures can run from 10-40 points depending on volatility.

FOREX Markets

Forex markets are the lowest priced opportunity, with an entry level of capital of about $500. If you are interested in getting into day trading but lack capital, the FOREX markets can be an option to consider in order to get started with day trading. Even though FOREX markets have smaller required minimum accounts, the same rules apply. Traders should not risk more than 1% of their capital on a single trade. If you have a $2,000 account, then the most you'll want to risk on a trade is $20. While FOREX markets might appeal to you because of the smaller minimums, this is an entirely different world, with its own lingo and so forth. That isn't to say that getting some experience in the FOREX markets might be a good idea before risking massive amounts of capital day trading stocks. It very well might be an option to consider in order to use a real testing ground for day trading. FOREX.com, TD Ameritrade, Charles Schwab, and ETrade are recommended brokers for FOREX. This market will require you to study international trade and to spend time analyzing the global economy, rather than focus on individual companies. It's really a different animal, however, it can be complementary, and many traders do both.

Why Day Trade Options

Day trading stocks have a high barrier for entry because of capital requirements. You may or may not already be in a position to do it, but if you're not trading options provide a low barrier to entry alternative. There are several reasons to trade options rather than stocks. To begin with, trading options don't require hardly any money at all (in comparison) and it will allow you to gain experience looking at many of the same underlying fundamentals that day trading stocks require – since they are ultimately based on the same market.

- Options can be cheap. You can trade options at a much lower premium price as compared to the price required to buy stocks.

- Options offer huge upside potential. The percentage gains in options can be orders of magnitude larger than gains in stocks. So, you can invest a smaller amount of money, and reap larger gains on a percentage basis.

- You don't have to exercise the option to profit from it.

- Volatility makes trading stocks risky; it can make trading options profitable.

- The low price required to invest in options contracts means that you can often put together a diverse portfolio, even when making short term trades.

- It may be harder to get competitive spreads with options while day trading.

There are some downsides to day trading options. One important factor is that when day trading options, time value may limit short term changes in price. Options are also less liquid than the underlying stocks, so that can mean wider bid-ask spreads. Trading options will require you to get the same basic knowledge of day trading that we covered when discussing stocks. Ultimately, the value of the option is determined by the value of the underlying asset – the stock price.

Things to watch day trading options

Let's take a look at some indicators specific to options that you'll want to pay close attention to.

- Put/Call Ratio. If this is high, that means more traders are investing in puts for the underlying asset. In other words, the outlook is bearish because more traders are betting against the underlying or shorting it.
- Money Flow Index. This helps identify overbought and oversold assets. It tells you the flow of money that goes into the underlying

asset or out of it over a specified period of time. Money flow takes into account both price and volume.

- Open Interest – this is the total number of outstanding options contracts that have not been settled.

- Relative strength and Bollinger bands (discussed in previous chapters).

Best Tools to Operate Day Trading

Day traders may have special needs to act fast and get information as quickly as possible in ways that normal stock investors don't require. One of the most important things a day trader needs is access to breaking news related to the markets. You're never going to get the kind of detailed and early news that the big players in the institutional investor world will get, but you can still opt for the best options, and that should include Benzinga breaking news.

In addition, some other tools you are going to need:

- Hotkeys, to execute trades quickly.
- Of course, you will need a laptop and a solid internet connection.
- Stock scanning software. Trade ideas are a solid tool: https://www.trade-ideas.com
- eSignal for specialized charting.
- Cable or satellite television, to keep up with ongoing financial news on finance channels like Fox Business and CNBC.
- TAS Market Profile – a software package designed specifically for day traders. See https://www.tasmarketprofile.com/

Chapter 6: How much do day traders make?

Day trading can sound exciting, and it certainly is. And if you have larger amounts of capital to invest, and you're very good at it, then day trading can help you make large amounts of money over short time periods. But if you are just getting started, how much can you really earn day trading? Let's try looking at some realistic scenarios before having visions of millions of dollars.

The first thing to consider when you are trying to gauge the potential for success in any endeavor is the Pareto principle. Basically, this principle tells us that 20% of the people get 80% of the spoils. It doesn't matter what you're talking about, you could be talking about farmers. In that case, 20% of the farmers will be responsible for 80% of the output. In the case of the stock market, 20% of the investors will take 80% of the returns, and this most certainly applies to day trading.

Most day traders are going to have to keep their day job, and many may end up losing their initial capital investment.

This isn't too out and out discouraging anyone from taking up day trading. There are many factors that will decide success or failure. For example, many people start off with high levels of excitement when taking on something new like day trading, but then they fizzle out very quickly. In short, they simply fail to put in the work required to excel. There could be a million reasons for it. Some people might wilt at the first sign of a challenge. Others may become bored with it. Some people are downright lazy – day trading actually takes work and they were hoping for a get rich quick scheme.

Just like only a small percentage of basketball players are ever going to be NBA stars, only a tiny percentage of day traders are going to rise to become the cream of the crop and make millions of dollars. That said, you can take action to seriously tip the odds in your favor.

After all, many people practice basketball with an all-out effort and become top-level players, even if they aren't Kobe Bryant or Lebron James, they still may be very successful. The same principle applies to day trading. You may be a budding star or not – but if you dive in 100% to study the markets and finance and trading – you will up your odds significantly and even if you don't become a star, if you are a smart trader who hedges risk well then you may be able to make a solidly upper-middle-class income from it even if you don't become a top level trader.

One rule is that disciplined traders, at least over the long run, are going to make more money than people who are flying by the seat of their pants kinds of people. The more capital you start with, the more money that you're going to make. But let's have a look at the minimum. Suppose that you start out with the recommended minimum amount of capital, which is $30,000.

Using leverage at 4:1, that means you can potentially control $120,000 worth of stock. Remember that there is a 1% rule on risk per trade and starting with $30,000 that means you'll be trading $300 at a time. Assuming you're a disciplined trader, you will have a good stop-loss strategy. Standard values are a win rate of 50% (that is half your trades are profitable) and your winners are around 1.5 times bigger than your losers. These numbers sound like no big deal, but it may take you a couple of years to get to this level. Now let's use these assumptions together with a guess that you make on average five trades per day or about 100 per month. With a 50% success rate, you'll have 50 profitable trades per month. A reasonable stop loss is $0.10, so with a 1.5 times ratio of the winner to loser you're making $0.15 per share in profits. You can control 3,000 shares per trade. So that gives you a monthly profit of $22,500. Your losses come from the stop loss figure of ten cents a share, so you're going to lose $15,000 per month.

Your gross income will then be the difference, or $7,500 a month. However, remember that you'll need to pay lots of commissions. Brokers don't let you trade stock for free. In the end, your actual profit will probably be about $5,000 a month.

Now, this isn't bad to get started. So, you're able to work from home, doing something fun and exciting that is even a little bit risky, and make an OK middle-class income from it. But it's probably not the kind of income you were hoping to see.

That isn't to say that you can't grow your business over time and make huge amounts of money. You absolutely can do that. However, what we're really trying to show here is that day trading really isn't a get rich quick scheme. It's not really different from any other kind of business that takes time, work, and energy to grow.

Of course, you might be better than average. If you are really good, maybe 65% of your trades turn out profitable and you're banking $8,000-$9,000 per month depending on the size of commissions you have to pay. That's not an unrealistic possibility, however, remember not everyone is as talented as anyone else. Some people are going to do worse than the 50% success rate that we initially started with, and in those cases, they will make less money, maybe a couple thousand a month or less. Still, more won't make anything, and some are going to end up with losses.

The point of this discussion isn't to discourage people, it's to get you going into this with your eyes wide open and having realistic expectations. There is no doubt a few people reading this who will master day trading and end up millionaires. We sincerely hope that you are that one person!

Conclusion

Thank you for taking the time to read *How to Trade Options: Day Trading Strategies.* If you found this book helpful, please jump on Amazon and give us a thoughtful review. Thanks again!

Day trading is not for everyone, and neither is trading options. However, trading options and doing day trading are both exciting endeavors. Once you get your feet wet investing in options, you may find the temptation of day trading calls. Normally, day trading stocks requires that you open an account with a brokerage with a large amount of upfront cash. In the United States, you're required to have a minimum of $25,000 in your account, and it's recommended that you have at least $30,000 in order to give you some cushion against losses. Losses during day trading are to be expected. It takes a long time and a lot of devotion to get good at day trading, and even the best and most experienced day traders can experience long losing streaks.

Options provide a great way to get into the markets while risking a lot less capital. With options, you can control large numbers of shares of stock for small amounts of money. You can exercise the option or not, giving you flexibility. Selling your option can give you a way to quickly profit when there are big stock moves, and profit margins with options are often much higher than they are with stocks.

Day trading can be an exciting opportunity. We recommend that you test the waters by using one of the stock trading simulators recommended in the book and then using your knowledge to day trade options contracts. Options are based on the underlying stock so everything that you learn about day trading stocks applies to options as well. If you want to learn about options I suggest reading my first book in this series, How to Trade Options which is a detailed book aimed at people who are just beginning with options.

Introduction

Congratulations on beginning your journey to greater wealth and financial independence!

Most people are very familiar with "normal" stock investing. You buy a diverse set of stocks – even better into a mutual fund or exchange-traded fund – and then hold onto them until retirement, when you start to slowly cash them out for income.

People are also familiar with day trading. When it comes to day trading, however, most people have a cartoonish view of it, believing that day trading is some kind of scam or get rich quick scheme where you try to make tens of thousands of dollars in a few hours. That really isn't true, day trading, while riskier than long term stock investments, is a disciplined and scientific approach to making money from stock trades. But it does require significantly more dedication in time, knowledge and effort than most people are willing or able to put into their investing activities.

What people don't know about is the glorious middle between these two possible ways to approach the stock market, and that's *swing trading*. This offers a type of middle in between day trading and long-term investing, where you can hold stocks for days or even a few months, in order to take advantage of some of the longer term growth that comes with good stocks, but also get some of the edges that day traders have. Swing trading provides are a more secure way to "play" the markets than day trading, and in fact, the reality is that swing traders often make far more money than day traders. You can also do swing trading in many cases without capital requirements or regulators breathing down your neck the way they might with day trading.

In this book, we'll introduce you to swing trading, and we're going to talk about swing trading with options. This is another way of investing that the "average Joe" isn't familiar with. We'll explain what options are and how to use the power of leverage options provide to make more profits and amazing ROI on your money. If you want a more detailed exposition on options, please see my first book in this series, How to Trade Options.

Chapter 1: Swing Trading – The Basics

Swing trading sounds suspicious, but as we'll see it's a solid middle-road type of investing in the stock market that will appeal to many people. Before we get into the specifics of what swing trading is, let's quickly discuss its evil twin, day trading. How does that work? Very briefly, day trading is a strategy that hopes to take advantage of a single day gain or loss. Some people see it as a "fast money" or "get rich quick" approach to stock market trading, but it's nothing of the sort. In order to engage in day trading, you must have an account with a minimum of $25,000 with a broker. So, if you're looking to make money on the stock market, but are short on cash, day trading isn't going to be something you can use to get rich.

Besides having a specific capital requirement, day trading requires active participation in the stock market that involves getting deeply invested in following financial news from many sources, trying to stay on top of rumors and breaking news, and watching every little move of your stocks throughout the day. You must do your due diligence with day trading. It also involves having some highly technical skills that most people who invest in the stock market would rather not bother with. The bottom line is that day trading is serious, and high-risk business. For our purposes, the key takeaway is that day trading attempts to leverage stock market gains (or losses, if you are shorting a stock) that occur within a single trading day. At the close, you're out of all your positions. This can be an advantage in that you avoid overnight risks, stocks can often take hits with trading on Asian and European markets.

We all know what long-term investing is. Basically, people try to set up a diverse portfolio of stocks (and other securities like bonds, mutual funds, etc.) in order to build long-term wealth. The definition of long-term might vary from person to person, it might be five years, ten years, or even three decades. Most people are probably thinking of building up some wealth over the course of their adult working years, so we are probably talking about a 25-30-year time window in most cases. Long-term investors may not even actively manage a portfolio, they might let a professional take care of that for them. If they do manage their own portfolio, they are going to invest using techniques like dollar cost averaging that minimize risks and take advantage of the average, longer-term behavior of the stock market. Over time, the trend of the stock market is up – and that is what people are after so they can build a 'nest egg'.

Some of us are more impatient, and, like the active involvement in the markets that day trading can provide. We love pouring over charts and graphs, studying companies and stock movements. Is there some kind of middle ground for these kinds of folks, who aren't up for day trading?

It turns out there is – and it's swing trading that we are after. Swing trading simply involves holding stocks for multiple days. One of the goals of swing trading is to give your investments some room for growth. With day trading, you're taking advantage of short-term gaps that increase the value of a stock. In swing trading, you're taking advantage of multi-day gaps up, so that you can build more gains from your investments. People think that day traders are the people who get rich on the stock market – and some do – but it's often swing traders who will make more money over the course of a year.

Since you're holding your investments for a bit longer, swing trading cuts down some of that risk that day traders have of making bad bets and incurring streaks of losses. So how long to swing traders hold their stocks?

It can vary quite a bit. Sometimes a swing trader will only hold a stock for a day or maybe two. But some swing traders hold stocks for 10 days, a month, 50 days, two months, or even out to 100 days (the definitions vary among swing traders – most would probably say 2 days up to a few weeks). You may completely hold onto a position, or you may sell a small part like 15% after 5 days and hold the rest for 30 days. There are more possibilities with swing trading.

Since you're holding your securities for a longer time period, you're exposing yourself to some risks that day traders aren't exposed to. For example, there can be short-term, dramatic events that can significantly influence stock prices over the course of a month or two. These could include war, terrorist attack, or even simply remarks from the President or The Fed. Swing traders are also more exposed to bad company news. Maybe the CEO gets arrested for corruption, or perhaps the company's product results in the deaths of some children. Swing traders, unlike day traders, hold their investments overnight, and so can be at a disadvantage when there are bad results in off-hours trading. These kinds of events are bad for all investors, but swing traders are more likely to take a negative hit from them than day traders. And long-term investors too – if you're holding stocks (and probably funds like the S&P 500) for anywhere from 5-30 years, those sorts of events often amount to background noise. Not so for the swing trader.

That said, in most cases swing trading provides a solid middle ground in between day trading and long-term investing that can help you grow wealth fast. Swing trading is also a bit slower paced than day trading. Many people view day trading as demanding, and that's a realistic perception. Swing trading is an alternative that lets people who like getting into the nitty-gritty of the markets but don't want the high pressure.

Of course, there are no guarantees in life, but let's start looking at the strategies employed by swing traders to help them earn profits.

How much capital do you need for swing trading

Unlike day trading, where brokers *require* you to have a minimum of $25,000 (and $30,000 is recommended) there aren't formal requirements for swing trading. Brokers pay special attention to day traders (and regulators do as well) but not so much for swing traders. That said, you will have to evaluate how much money you need to invest in order to reach your goals. But you can start small to get started if you like and remember that options trading lets you leverage a lot more power over the markets with smaller investments, so trading options is one way you can reduce your initial capital requirements.

However, a general rule of thumb according to market experts is that you should have around $10,000 in your account if you are a swing trader. Moreover, you should only risk 1% in a single trade, which for $10,000 would be $100. If you are more of a risk taker, you could risk up to 2%. You can manage your risk using stop-loss orders, which we will talk about below. The risk of a security losing value is called downside risk.

When it comes to minimum capital requirements, the following rules apply:

- A day trader is someone who makes more than 4 trades a week that open and closes on the same day.
- A day trader must have $25,000 in their account.
- There are no minimum requirements for swing trader accounts.
- However, if you cross that line of more than 4 trades a week that open and close on the same day, you'll be labeled a day trader and be forced to follow the rules for day traders.
- Swing traders have 2x leverage. So, if you invest $10,000, you can buy $20,000 worth of stock. Use leverage carefully, however. If you lose on your trades, you can end up owing more than what's in the account.
- When you're trading, you need to worry about commissions, not just the loss or gain on the

stock. You should risk at least $100 on a trade to deal with commissions. Otherwise, they will eat up your profits or magnify your losses.

The way risk works

It's important to understand how traders evaluate risk. Some readers may misunderstand, thinking that when we say that you can risk $100 if you have a $10,000 account, that means you take your $100 and try to find a share or a few shares to buy. That isn't how it works.

First, you put in a stop-loss order. This is an order that you place after buying a stock that puts in an automatic sell order on your behalf if the stock price drops below a specific level. If we buy 10 shares of XYZ stock for $100 each, which will cost in total $1,000 (ignoring commissions, for the sake of simplicity), say we will place a stop-loss order of $90. This means that if the XYZ stock drops to $90 a share, our shares are automatically sold and we lost $10 a share, for a total loss of $100. If the stock is rapidly dropping, maybe it dropped to $85 a share. So, a stop-loss order is a type of insurance in the stock market, that prevents you from losing your shirt. It's also helpful for people who can't be in front of the computer all day long managing their investments – that way you have some automatic protection built in if things go south while you're not there. If you didn't place a stop-loss order and for some reason XYZ really tanked, you could end up losing a huge amount of money.

So, we see that the actual risk that we're talking about is going to be determined by looking at the price per share minus the amount we specify on the stop-loss order. Let's summarize:

- If a share is going for $200, and you place a stop-loss order of $180, the trade risk is $20.
- That means the amount you are willing to risk on a trade of 10 shares is $20 x 10 = $200. This is the account risk.

- If you have a $10,000 trading account, then your risk is 2%, since 0.02 x $10,000 = $200.

How much you risk is up to you, but these types of conservative figures are given because it's entirely possible that you're going to make multiple bad trades all right in a row. Of course, we're giving examples that aren't going to fit every situation. You can also minimize risk to different levels. In fact, more active traders put more stringent limits on risk than long-term investors do. The reason why is the following.

A stop-loss order has a risk of its own. Throughout the day, stock prices fluctuate a lot, and it has a random pattern over the short term that looks chaotic. So even if a stock is set to increase in value over the case of a day or a couple of days, over shorter time periods it may have some downturns in price. The risk is that one of these random fluctuations could drop the price at or below the limit you specify on the stop-loss order, and your shares will be sold. But then the stock climbs right back up. Day traders are concerned with fluctuations of the stock over the short term, so put tighter limits. As a swing trader, you might be planning on holding the stock for some time, but a lot less than a year. There could be longer-term trends that might trigger a stop-loss even though you're planning on holding the stock.

To see how this works, let's suppose that you bought some shares of Apple on 12/18/18, at $166.07 per share. We could put a stop-loss order on that of 5% to minimize our risk. Since 5% of $166.07 is $8.30, our stop-loss order will go in effect if the price drops below $157.77. That happened on December 20, when it dropped to $156.83. Our shares would have been sold. The stock bounced around a little and even dropped to $142 after New Year's so we might have felt good about ourselves at that point. However, by 3/21/19, the stock had climbed back up to $194.09. So, we missed out...

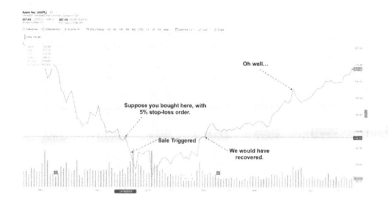

The bottom lines. You should use stop-loss orders. You need to protect yourself against losses so that you don't lose your shirt. But think about them carefully. The shorter time period over which you intend to hold the stock, the smaller the percentage you should be willing to risk, and vice versa. So, a day trader might use 1-5% while a long-term investor might use 15%. You will have to use a level that you're comfortable with. You'll have to sit down with each trade you make and calculate how much money you are willing to lose on the deal and then set your stop loss accordingly. Sometimes you're going to be wrong and miss out on a rebound but that's life. Now let's learn some basic concepts that are important in swing trading.

Trends

A big part of swing trading is recognizing trends in stocks, whether they are up or down. We will also want to look for points at which the trend will reverse. This works no matter how you're trading. If you are looking for long investments, then you're looking for the end of a downturn for buying opportunities, and peaks for selling opportunities. In other words, we are looking to buy low and sell high. If you are shorting the stock, then you'll be looking at the opposite trends.

Swing Traders Use Trends

To make money swing trading, you're going to utilize trends in order to get into a stock and determine when to exit the stock and book your profits. You are seeking to take advantage of a single move in the stock or a "swing" in the stock price. When a stock swings, then that means the opposing pressure is about to take over. So, you may be looking to exit your position. Alternatively, you may be looking for a good buying opportunity. In the next chapter, we will look at indicators of changing trends. The bottom line is that swing traders usually go with the prevailing trend. If you're bullish, you look for upward trends in the stock and book your profits on the upside. If you're bearish, then you're looking to capture gains on the downside.

Chapter 2: Swing Trading Indicators

Swing trading relies on using several indicators to spot changing trends in a share price. We use these indicators to determine when it's a good time to buy and sell our securities. These will be points at which the stock market is signaling through buying and selling of large numbers of traders and institutional investors that demand is overwhelming people selling off or the desire to get out of a stock is overwhelming new buyers. Depending on whether you are investing in calls or puts these are times to either get in or out of an investment.

Support and Resistance

While swing trading isn't as fast paced as day trading, we're going to want to look for turning points in the market. The goal is to be able to spot price reversals before they get fully underway. This could be a buying or selling opportunity depending on the situation and how you're investing.

- Support: Support is a lower boundary on a stock
  – it's a price level that the share price doesn't
  drop below for a given period of time (over the
  long term, anything can happen). In other
  words, it's a lower limit to the stock price. If
  you're spotting support in a stock chart, then
  that is a time to buy if you are hoping to go long
  on the stock (i.e. hold it for a while until it rises
  enough that you can book some profits by
  selling). Support indicates that the stock is
  probably going to go up in price because buyers
  are starting to enter the stock and buying up the
  stock is starting to overcome selling pressure.

- Resistance: This is an upper bound to a share
  price that the stock doesn't seem able to rise
  above. If you're long on a stock, resistance
  indicates this is probably a good time to sell and
  book your profits. This is a time at which people
  are starting to get out of stock. Put another way,
  selling is starting to overcome buying pressure.

Basic supply and demand concepts lie behind support and resistance. Suppose that a stock's price has been dropping. As the price drops, unless there is something major going on (like say, the CEO being arrested or the company going bankrupt) then as prices fall, demand will start to increase. Support happens at a critical mass when buyers start to match in number against sellers, so the price stops dropping. This is a good indicator that the price will probably start going up. You can find periods of support by drawing a straight line through the lowest lows over the time period. Rising demand causes to support and will start to cause rising prices.

Resistance works the same way but in the opposite direction. It's caused by declining demand. For whatever reason, the price of a stock has been going up and now traders are thinking they want to get out. If you've bought the stock at a lower price and you've been hoping to make profits, now is probably a good time to do so.

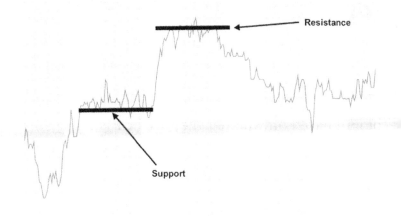

If the share price goes below the support or above a resistance price level, then they switch roles. That is, suppose that a stock has been bouncing around a support level of $45. If $45 is the support level, the share price hasn't dropped below that. But suppose it drops to $42. That indicates the stock will be going lower, so now we consider $45 to be a resistance.

Of course, these are guidelines, they are not absolute rules.

What is a candlestick

Most people are used to seeing line charts of the stock market, but traders rely on candlesticks. You will see candlesticks on specialized stock charts, and they are colored based on whether they are bearish or bullish. The thick mid-section represents the open and closing price. The longer the candlestick body, the bigger the difference between open and closing prices. Thin "wicks" or shadows emanating from the candlestick represent the highs and the lows that occurred between opening and closing. Charts can be displayed for differing time periods so a candlestick might represent a day, or five minutes, or one minute. Candlesticks originated from Japanese rice merchants who used them to keep track of changing rice prices on the markets.

A bearish candlestick is either red in color, or if the chart is black & white it's solid black. A bullish candlestick is green in color. Candlesticks contain a lot of information and it's important to understand what they represent to understand what is happening in the markets. This is a bearish candlestick:

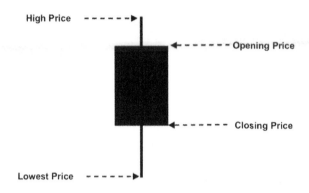

This is a bullish candlestick:

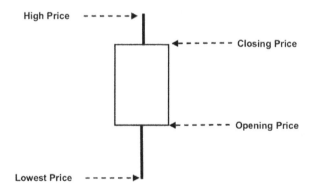

The length of the candlestick indicates the pressure. So, a long bullish candlestick (green in color charts) indicates strong buying pressure. A long bearish candlestick (red on color charts) indicates strong selling pressure.

Indecision Candlesticks

Traders need to look for indecision candlesticks. These have narrow or skinny bodies and long wicks. They are sometimes called "dojis" as they were known in the Japanese markets. Indecision candlesticks represent the possibility of a changing trend in the market. Indecision candlesticks are informative but must be considered together with the trend they are incorporated in, but they are often found at the top or bottom of a trend. However, indecision candlesticks don't always represent a coming change, so you use them in context with other ways to evaluate what is going on. Here is an example of an indecision candle.

If the top wick is much longer than the bottom wick, this is called a "shooting star". A shooting star that is found at the top of an uptrend can be a bearish signal. If you are in a long position, it can indicate that this is a good time to sell. If you are shorting or investing in puts, it might be a good time to get in the market.

If you see a very long wick on the top with little or no wick coming out of the bottom, and the candlestick is at the bottom of a downward trend, that is an inverted hammer. This may be a bullish signal. It could indicate that the trend may be reversing and prices are about to rise.

Another concept you want to think about when looking at candles is engulfing. What this means is that a candle in a given position has a larger body than the previous candle, and they are opposite types. Two examples to pay attention to are seeing several red candles in a row in a downward trend, with the last red candle engulfed by a green (bullish) candle. This can possibly represent a coming upturn in the share price so it may represent a buying opportunity for long positions. Conversely, if you are looking at an upward trend, and green candles are engulfed by a red (bearish) candle, that might mean that the stock price will soon turn downward. That could be a signal you could interpret to mean it's a good time to buy puts or short the stock. If you are in a long position, that is a good time to sell.

Uptrends

Bullish swing traders look for uptrends. Over the short term, stocks move up and down a lot, but this short-term up and down movement is random and takes place within a larger trend that may be straight up or straight down. In other words, there is a kind of zigzag pattern that is inside some overall trend. For example, we can see this type of movement in a 3-month chart of Google stock. The chart is clearly trending up with time but bounces around a bit on the way up.

We know the stock is in an uptrend when linking together the shorter-term zigzag patterns they fit together pointing toward a higher stock price, as seen with Google over the displayed time period. However, countertrends will occur when a stock is moving in a larger uptrend. A swing trader wants to look for these countertrends to spot opportunities for investment. What you want to see is evidence of an uptrend that then runs into resistance. This can produce a countertrend. So, if the stock is in a long term upward

247

rise, the countertrend will be a small downturn followed by some sideways movement. You look for the stock to begin an upward trend again, and a good time to enter the market is at this point when the stock is resuming its long march upward. In the chart below, the dotted line represents the overall upward trend. We see that in the midst of the overall trend, there is a short-term countertrend during which the stock price drops, where it languishes a little with support. Then the stock begins to resume its longer term trend which is upward. This can be a good place to buy, then you can hold the stock until you see a solid resistance signal and sell to book your profits.

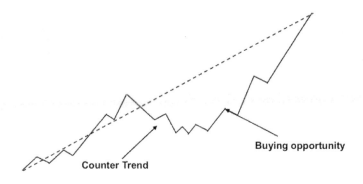

Counter Trend

Buying opportunity

Using One-Cancels-Other Orders

A one-cancel-other order is a great tool for swing traders. This allows you to lock in sale prices for price rise or a price drop. To understand how this works, you need to know what a limit order is. Simply put, a limit order is an instruction to the broker to sell your shares if the price meets the limit or goes higher. So for this example, the limit order is your profit taking price. Of course, it's possible you might miss out on further gains in the share price, this is a risk you take using this strategy, and it's not for everyone. But the way this type of order works, is you specify a profit-taking price and a stop loss price, setting bounds on what's acceptable to you in the trade. If the condition for one of the orders is met, then the other order will be canceled. These are sometimes known as OCO orders.

A bullish swing trader can use an OCO order to their advantage when a stock has been going up for several days, and then it's a countertrend, followed by support. Then wait for the beginning of the upward trend to resume and place your order. A good place to look for entering your position is when the stock goes higher than the previous day's low.

Let's suppose that you buy XYZ stock at $40 a share, and it's been in a fairly long-term uptrend. You can use the bottom of the previous support to set a stop loss price, say it was $38. We can take our profit-taking price to be $45. If the price enters a downturn again, and it drops to $37.75, our shares are sold since the stop-loss order was triggered, and the price taking order is canceled. On the other hand, if the price continues the long-term trend upward and hits $45, then we take our profit and the stop loss order is canceled. Using this type of order, we are able to get what we want out of the trade without having to spend all day in front of the computer watching the stock. Traders who are more actively involved may wish to keep a closer eye on the stock and look for selling signals.

Bearish Strategy

A similar strategy can be used for bearish traders. In this case, we'd be looking at a downward trend that lasts for several days. There may be a countertrend, or the stock may simply hit support with a sideways movement for a time. Then you look for it to resume the downward trend. You are looking to enter your position when the stock drops below the previous day's low. A bearish trader will look to use a sell-stop-limit order. So, you will borrow shares from the broker and immediately sell them. When the price drops to a level where you can take profits, then you buy them back and return them to the broker. Note the stock is in a downward trend. The difference between your selling price and the price at which you bought the shares back is your profit (not counting commissions).

Fading

Most swing traders go with the prevailing trend. However, you can also use fading, which is looking to take advantage of the countertrend. A bearish trader who is looking to fade wants to get in at the high of the swing, in the expectation that the stock is going to drop. You short the stock at the high or buy puts. A bullish trader will look to get in at the stock low and buy calls or buy shares waiting for the next upturn.

Bull Flags

A bull flag is another way to take advantage of the momentum of a stock. As a swing trader, you'll be looking for bull flag signals on a daily stock chart, and not in the short term the way a day trader would. A bull flag is characterized by a short-term major rise in the stock. So, you will see a nearly vertical increase in the stock price. Prices will rise a certain amount, and then there will be a pullback, where the price moves sideways for a while. The rapid rise followed by the pullback gives a flag pattern in the stock chart. The hope here is that following the "flag" pattern, there will be a breakout to a higher stock price where you can take your profits. Volume is a strong indicator with bull flags. You should look for a strong volume signal that comes with a sharp rise in prices. There should also be some sort of external signals, such as a major company announcement or something in the news. Set your stop-loss at just below the sideways pullback price level. It's also possible to use an OCO order here. You can set your stop loss and a limit order where you'll take your profits. The profit target per share should be a 2:1 reward to risk level. So, if you risk $1, then you should set your limit order such that your profit is $2.

Bear Flag

For the bearish trader, there is the bear flag, which is a similar pattern in reverse. In this case, there is a strong downward trend in the share price, followed by a sideways movement or pullback, setting up support. Again, there should be a large volume and hopefully, there is some external news that led to the sudden selloff in shares. In this case, you are looking for it to resume a downward trend. As a swing trader, you're looking at daily charts for flag signals, you're not going to be working them as a day trader.

Spotting Reversals

We can use candlesticks to look for potential reversals when the trend of the stock suddenly shifts to move in the opposite direction. A reversal is going to be different from having the stop drop down, hit support, and possibly go up afterward. A reversal is going to be an abrupt change. Engulfing candlesticks can be a signal of a reversal. Look at the body of a candlestick that is a different color/type than the previous candlestick. So, this could be the appearance of a bearish or red candlestick after many green or bullish candlesticks that have come with an upward trend in price. If the bearish candlestick engulfs the green candlesticks that came before it, this can be taken as a reversal signal. The strength of a reversal signal is determined by the size of the reversal candlestick body. If it's larger, that is a stronger signal and more of an indication that you may want to enter a trade. If we are looking at a bearish candlestick, then we have an opportunity to short stock or to buy puts.

On the other hand, when we see a stock going down with several red or bearish candlesticks in succession, and then there is the sudden appearance of a green or bullish candlestick, that may be an indication of a reversal that will lead to rising share prices. The same criteria apply here, we are looking for a bullish candlestick that engulfs the previous bearish candlestick. This can be an indication that many buyers are starting to see the stock as something they want to get into. Therefore, it may be an opportunity to go long or buy calls.

One candlestick isn't a trend, so look for several candlesticks that go in a row to make a trend upward or downward, followed by an engulfing candlestick of the opposite variety.

Sometimes indecision candlesticks can precede a reversal. So rather than seeing multiple candlesticks of one type followed by an engulfing candlestick, you may see the appearance of some indecision candlesticks prior to the change.

Moving Averages

Moving averages are an important tool to be aware of as a swing trader. Traders are using them en masse, so a moving average provides a way for you to "go with the crowd", which can be a good idea since trends in price changes are nothing more than lots of traders making the same moves. There are two types of moving averages that you need to think about. The first type is called the EMA. This means an exponential moving average. As you can deduct from the word exponential, this is a fast-moving average. An exponential moving average gives more weight to recent price changes, and it will reflect these changes rapidly. One downside of this is that the EMA is also more likely to give wrong information going forward because it's too sensitive to these recent price changes. There are also SMA or simple moving averages. These are slower than exponential moving averages. When there is a price change, it's going to take longer to see it reflected in the SMA than in the EMA. Both tools are useful, but swing traders are in their positions longer than day traders, so the EMA is of more interest to day traders generally than the SMA, while for swing traders the SMA is more useful. Day traders who are looking for quick gains or shorts are more interested in the type of information the EMA can provide them because you're interested in the short-term price movements. A swing trader isn't interested in the short-term price movements and zigzag behavior. So, the SMA provides a smoothed-out average that is more useful for the swing trader. You can look at different moving averages (besides the type) by looking at the period length. Swing traders want to smooth out the noise in the stock market and avoid premature signals. The moving averages that swing traders are interested in are those with higher periods. The more periods, the longer the time period of price action that will be incorporated into the moving average. This is also something that will correlate with the length of your trades, if you are going to hold your position for a shorter time period, then you'll want fewer periods in your moving average. Swing traders, in particular, are looking for a compromise between long term moving averages and short-term moving averages. For that reason, the standard chosen by most swing traders is the 50-period moving average. However, this is not the only option of interest to swing traders. You're going to be interested in other indicators like supports, resistance, and trends, and different moving averages can help you in that regard. For trends, use a 20-period moving average. A 100-period moving average will help with support and resistance. It's also good for doing analysis on a daily or weekly basis. If you want one year of price action with daily charts, you can use a 200 or 250 period moving average.

Looking at the 21 period EMA, you are going to find that it fits upward and downward trends nicely.

Beginners will probably want to stick with one moving average until you gain some experience working with livestock charts, and a beginning swing trader should probably look at the 50 periods moving average. However, it's possible to have one stock chart with many moving averages and this provides a lot of information so you will want to use it. Faster moving averages are colored in red on stock charts. Swing traders can also use 10-period exponential moving averages for trend signals. When you're swing trading, you want to be trading with the trend unless you're fading. If a stock is trading above the 10-day EMA, then this is a buy signal for an upward trend. If the stock is trading below the 10-day EMA, this is a sell signal. You can use the 20/21 period EMA for this purpose as well. Again, if the trading is above the 21 periods EMA, this is a buying signal. If it's trading below the 21 periods EMA, that is a selling signal.

Golden and Death Crosses

For the swing trader, golden and death crosses are important to use for spotting long term signals. A golden cross occurs when a short term moving average crosses a long-term moving average (that is the short-term moving average goes above the long-term moving average). Swing traders will watch the 200-day moving average and 50-day moving average. The golden cross will happen when the 50-day moving average crosses and goes above the 200-day moving average. This is a bullish signal. You want to enter a long position when the 50-day average goes above your 200 days moving average.

The opposite type of crossing is called a death cross. In that case, the 50-day moving average drops below the 200 days moving average. This is a signal the stock is going to enter a downward trend. So this is a bearish signal, and the 50-day moving average crossing to move below the 200 days moving average either means you should sell your position if you are long or if you are bearish then you'll want to short the stock or buy puts.

When looking at golden and death crosses, check trading volume. High trading volume is a data point that supports what the cross is telling you. Always confirm a golden cross or death cross with other trading signals. While they are quite reliable, golden and death crosses often lead to false signals.

Caution for ranges

A range is when the share price is moving about between a support and a resistance. If this is happening, then you will want to ignore the moving averages for the time being. They will not provide you with useful information in this situation and could mislead you possibly leading to trading losses.

Bollinger Bands

Bollinger bands use standard deviation calculations to provide an envelope around stock prices, measuring market volatility and giving indications where support and resistance may lie. There are three things that you can glean information about from Bollinger bands:

- Volatility (how much the price is fluctuating up and down).
- The extent of price movement.
- Trend lines that define support and resistance.

There are formulas for Bollinger bands, but I'm confident that most readers aren't really that interested in the formulas themselves, and only interested in getting an idea of what Bollinger bands can do to help your trading strategies. Bollinger bands are calculated relative to a moving average. So, you will want to use a moving average of relevance to swing trading like a 21 day or 50 days moving average. The Bollinger band is going to give you information on the spread of prices about that moving average. The information is calculated by using closing prices over a given time period.

You will see Bollinger bands displayed on stock charts encompassing the candlesticks. You'll want to see how wide or narrow they are about the actual stock prices. If the bands are narrowed, then that means that prices are less volatile and staying fairly close to one another over a small range. Wide Bollinger bands indicate more volatility. The closing prices for each period will be divergent.

Bollinger bands can give use to buy and sell signals by indicating whether a stock is oversold or overbought. For this information, you'll want to see how the wicks of the candlesticks relate to the Bollinger bands. An oversold stock indicates a buying signal, and this is indicated when the wick of a candlestick touches the Bollinger band below. We look to the upper Bollinger band for selling signals and again look at the upper wick of the candlesticks. If the wick touches or crosses the upper Bollinger band, that is a signal the stock is overbought. In that case, you will want to sell.

Like all technical signals, you will want to take it with a grain of salt until you find supporting confirmation from other signals.

Candlesticks hitting the Bollinger bands can indicate a reversal (we were talking about wicks above, now we are talking about candlesticks). A hammer at the bottom of a Bollinger band after a downturn can be an indication that a downturn is about to reverse into an upward trend. Looking at the upward Bollinger band above the moving average, considered an upward trend, if you see a shooting star touching the band this may be indicating a reversal and a coming downward trend.

ABCD Strategy

This is a basic strategy that is often used by day traders. Swing traders can also use ABCD strategies but over the longer time periods, that swing traders focus on. What is doing is looking for patterns in the movements of the stock in order to get ideas about longer-term trends. A basic ABCD pattern begins with an upward trend to point A, followed by a countertrend to point B. The trader is looking for a breakout signal, which could occur if the price level goes above the point A after the countertrend. Peaks that drop off into a countertrend in the midst of an overall upward trend may do so because large numbers of traders were happy with their profits and so closed their positions. Of course, it's important not to look at stock charts in a complete vacuum. So, if there was bad news that hit the markets when there was a drop off from point A in the chart, then this analysis wouldn't apply, and you might not expect any upturn in the near future.

An ABCD pattern can be bearish or bullish, depending on where the ending point of the chart lies. This chart shown here is bearish when you are at the point D in the chart. Between points B and C, there are plenty of buying opportunities. For a swing trader, we are looking for this pattern occurring over the time of more than one day, it could even be a longer-term trend. A day trader is hoping to enter the position at point C and then exit the position at point D, on the same day. For a swing trader, this type of pattern might be over days, weeks or longer.

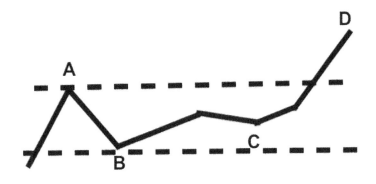

Let's suppose that ABC company closes at point A on Monday, which is $45 a share. At opening the following day, it drops to B at $35 a share, but by close the second day it's approaching point C which is $38 a share. A swing trader may enter their position if hoping for an upward trend if there are other signals to confirm. The next morning the stock opens and enters a strong upward trend, reaching point D at $55 a share. The support price level defined by point B $35 a share could have been taken as the stop loss. If an OCO approach were used, the trader could have set a limit order for $50 a share and booked a profit when the price went above it. Since we aren't day trading, we would not have to worry if the stock didn't quite reach that level right away. A swing trader would be comfortable holding the security for several days, or even weeks or a month or more waiting to see what the price did and giving the stock room to grow if it's a part of a larger trend for this security.

Bullish ABCD patterns can be seen as well when the stock is showing a downward trend. This provides alternatives for bearish investors as well, who may be looking at investing in puts early in the downturn. The bullish investor will be seeking signals of an upward trend after the stock bottoms out at point D.

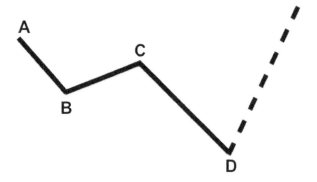

In an ABCD pattern, the lines A-B and C-D are called the legs. When there is a temporary reversal in the price of a stock against the long-term trend, we say that this is a retracement. This is also the countertrend discussed earlier. On the other hand, a correction is a real downturn in the stock price that is significant and represents the market bringing the stock price back down to a level that is either more consistent with the underlying fundamentals or due to news or overall trends in the market. The line B-C is a retracement or a correction.

Chapter 3: A Review of Options

An *option* is a type of contract. There are many types of contracts that are options, not just on the stock market. A typical example that is given to illustrate the use of options is a couple wants to buy a house in a newly developed area, but they want to see if other changes are made to the area such as the promised construction of a nearby school. So, they give the developer a $10,000 deposit for the option to buy a home in the development for $250,000 within six months. An arrangement is a contract, so if another buyer comes and offers the developer $350,000 for the same house while the contract is still in effect, the developer cannot sell the house to the second buyer. However, the first couple has the option of exercising their right to buy the house on or before the contract expires. Let's say the school they are hoping will be built is approved by the city government and construction begins. So, they decide to go ahead with the purchase. The developer must sell them the house for $250,000 and they move in. He has to sell them the house for $250,000 no matter what the market is doing, so for example if the construction of the school increased demand for homes in the area and prices have risen to $300,000, it doesn't matter, the developer has to sell the house at the pre-arranged price of $250,000. Now on the other hand, if the school was canceled and the couple decided not to buy the house, the developer can keep the $10,000 deposit, and then once the contract expires, he can sell the house to someone else for $350,000. The developer was obligated to carry out the terms of the contract, while the couple had the option to exercise their right to buy the house, or not.

Another example of an option is more common in daily life. That is a coupon. Of course, you don't always pay for coupons, but they give you the option to take an offer by a store. For example, a furniture store might offer a dining room set for 25% off over a limited time period. There is an expiration date and the person with the coupon has the option to exercise their right to buy the product at the offered price, or not.

Stock options work in much the same way. An option is a contract about underlying shares of stock. A seller writes the option, which comes with an expiration date. The option is sold for a price which is called the premium. Each option contract represents 100 shares of stock, and the premium is quoted on a per share basis. So, if you hear that the premium is $4, you will have to pay $4 x 100 shares = $400 for the options contract. The option in the contract is that you will have the right to buy or sell shares. The shares of stock that the contract is about are called the underlying. A major part of an option contract is setting a pre-arranged price for the stock, this is called the strike price. Most options last for three months, so you are agreeing to a price for the stock that must be honored over the entire life of the option contract.

There are two types of options:

- Calls: A call is an option to buy stock.
- Puts: A put is an option to sell a stock.

A call is an option for a long position. So, you'll buy a call option if you believe that the market price of the stock will rise above the strike price. In that case, you'll get a bargain price for the shares. Let's say that you are bullish on XYZ stock, which is trading at $50 a share. You buy a call with a strike price of $55. The price of the call is the premium, which we'll say is $5, so the total cost of the call is $5 x 100 = $500. Your analysis holds true, and XYZ spikes in price 30 days after you've bought the option contract to $70 a share after XYZ announces a snazzy new smartphone. The seller of the call must sell you 100 shares of XYZ at $55 a share, so you're "in the money" at $70 a share. You buy the shares for $55 and then you can sell them immediately for $70 a share. Your profit per share is the sales price minus the strike price minus the premium:

$70 - $55 -$5 = $10 per share

Of course, you'd have to pay a commission to the broker for the trades as well.

The seller of the call didn't do all that badly. Even though they didn't get the benefit of being able to sell at $70 a share, they were able to sell the shares at $55 and make a profit as compared to the $50 a share they were trading at when you entered the contract. However, the main reason the seller of the call would go for a deal like this is to get the premium, which is a way to leverage your stocks to get income. When you write a call contract and its stock that you currently own, that is called a covered call.

You can write a call on stocks you don't own. That's a naked call. However, if the buyer exercises their right to buy the shares, you've got to come up with them. In the scenario described here, you'd be in serious trouble. Since you didn't own the shares, you'd have to buy shares at $70 a share and sell them to the buyer of the call for $55 a share since that was the agreed upon strike price. In other words, you'd lose $15 x 100 = $1,500. Your loss would be partially offset by the $500 premium.

Now let's look at puts. This is an option to sell a stock. ABC is trading at $50 a share, but you're bearish on the stock. You buy a put for $5 a share, with a strike price of $40. Before the contract expires, the stock crashes on bad news to $20. So, you buy 100 shares at $20 a share. The seller of the put contract has to meet their obligation, so they are forced to buy the shares from you at the strike price, which was $40 a share. So, on a per share basis, you made (not including commissions):

$40 - $20 - $5 = $15 per share

To summarize, you pay a premium for the right but not the obligation to buy stocks when you buy a call. Or you pay a premium for the right but not the obligation to sell stocks when you buy a put.

People who own shares of stocks sell calls and puts to generate income. As we described above, a covered call is the safest way to sell options. By selling covered calls you can generate income from shares of stock you own.

All options contracts have an expiration date, which is typically the third Friday of the month. You can look at options tickers to see what the expiration date is. An option has more value the further it is from the expiration date, and it loses value the closer the contract gets to the expiration. The reason is that if the stock price hasn't passed the strike price, then the less time there is remaining on the contract the less time is available for the stock to move in order for the option to be exercised. The value of the option and the time remaining until the expiration date is captured in the concept of time value.

Options are cheaper than the stocks underlying the options contract. So, this is a way for traders to leverage stocks because when you buy options contracts you essentially control 100 shares of stock even if you don't currently own them. We've discussed how you can use options to profit by exercising them in this chapter. However, only about 12% of option contracts are actually exercised. Many simply expire worthlessly. In other words, if you reach the expiration date for the option, if the share price has not met the strike price the contract isn't worth anything (and actually strike price + the premium, otherwise the trade would not be profitable). The seller keeps the premium no matter what, so walks away from a worthless contract with the premium in their pocket.

Besides expiring worthless or being exercised, the third option for options is to trade them. In fact, that is what happens to most options, they are traded on options markets. In the next chapter, we will discuss trading options and how you can profit from that.

Chapter 4: Options Trading

Options contracts on stocks can be bought and sold, in other words, they can be traded. This is where some people get confused (if they weren't confused already). An option is a contract over underlying stock. The value of the option is related to the value of the underlying. However, the option has value in and of itself. People are interested in trading the options themselves, and this is where you can make good profits without having to actually exercise the options and buy and sell the underlying stocks (although you could do that as well if you wanted to). The return on investment or ROI for options is far higher than it is for stocks. We will illustrate this with some examples. So, some advantage of options trading includes:

- It's far cheaper to buy options than it would be to purchase the underlying stock.
- When the price of a stock appreciates, the value of an option goes up as well. If you owned the

stock, you would be able to sell it for a profit. However, as we'll see, you can make a much higher ROI on options than you can on stocks.

- One difference between stocks and options is that stocks don't have an expiration date. Options come with an expiration date. As the option gets closer to the expiration date, it's not worth as much because time will be running out on the ability to trade the option or to exercise the rights that come with the option should the stock reach the strike price. There is also less probability that the stock price will move past the strike price and be profitable as time is running out on the contract.

- Options contracts typically last for three months. However, there are other types of options with shorter expiration dates known as weekly and minis.

Options can be thought of as a type of insurance. This is one reason why investors will buy puts. If you own a stock that is $100 a share, you could buy a put at $95 a share, so that if the stock crashed to say $60 a share, you would be able to sell your shares for $95 a share, the pre-arranged strike price.

You don't have to hold an option to the expiration date. The movement of the stock price may make you want to sell the option before the expiration date. We will explain this in a bit.

Calls: In the Money and Out of the Money

The relationship between the strike price and the current stock market price of the underlying stock has a big influence on the price of the option. As the stock market price changes, the price of the option will change as well. When we say an option is "in the money" this means that the option could be exercised, and you would make a profit. For a call, that means that the strike price is less than the share price of the stock. So, you could exercise the option of buying the shares at the strike price, and then sell the shares on the open market for a higher price. Alternatively, if the option was in the money, you could simply trade the option itself, so sell it.

Let's say for an example that stock XYZ is trading at $100 a share. Call options will be available for many different strike prices, but we'll say that there are 7 available for our simple example, three strike prices below the current market price of $100 a share, one at $100 a share, and three at strike prices that are above $100 a share.

If the option expires, the three contracts with strike prices above the share price would be worthless. However, as long as there is still time on the contract, they are still worth money. The reason is that before the contract expires, the stock could still move in a direction to turn the worthless contracts from *out of the money* to *in the money*.

Let's say that the option with the $100 strike price (which happens to now match the share price) at 30 days to expiration is $5. Remember, that is the price per share, and there are 100 shares per option contract. So, the premium you have to pay to buy that options contract is $5 x 100 = $500. Options contracts with a strike price that is below $100 will cost more than $5. Suppose we have:

- Strike Price $90. This option is currently trading at $7, so total price is $7 x 100 = $700.
- Strike Price $80. This option is trading at $10, the total price of $1,000.
- Strike Price $60. This option is trading at $20, the total price of $2,000.

The further below the share price the strike price for an in the money call option is, the more it's worth. If you had bought the second option with the strike price of $80, and at the time the share price was close to the strike price, then when you bought the option it was probably quite a bit cheaper since now the stock is trading at $20 over the strike price. Let's say for the sake of example that you bought the option a month earlier for $600. So, you could sell the option now for $1,000, earning a $400 profit on your $600 investment. All three of the options contracts above are "in the money" call options because the strike price is currently below the share price. Now if the share price dropped to $88, then the first option with the strike price of $90 would be out of the money because the strike price would be above the share price. As a result, the premium for the option would drop. Remember – stock prices are currently changing, and the price of the option is dependent on the price of the underlying stock and moves with it (that is why this type of contract is sometimes called a derivative, the price is derived from the underlying asset behind the contract).

For our example, we also have three out of the money call options, that have strike prices above the share price. They are still worth some money because the stock could move to overtake them. The further above the share price the stock price is, however, the less the option is worth. Suppose we had these three options contracts:

- Strike Price $110. This option is currently trading at $3, so total price is $3 x 100 = $300.
- Strike Price $120. This option is trading at $2, total price $200.
- Strike Price $140. This option is trading at $0.25, a total price $25.

If the option expires, all three contracts would be worthless, because you could not exercise the option to buy the shares.

Put contracts are priced in the opposite manner. A put is in the money if the strike price is above the share price. On the other hand, if the strike price is below the share price, then the put is out of the money. Again, we will use the same example with the same share price of $100. For the put contracts, the three contracts with strike prices above $100 are in the money, and the higher the share price the more in the money they are (so we are imagining that when the contracts were written, the share price was above $140).

- Strike Price $110. This option is currently trading at $10, so total price is $10 x 100 = $1,000.
- Strike Price $120. This option is trading at $20, the total price of $2,000.
- Strike Price $140. This option is trading at $30, the total price of $3,000.

The put contracts with strike prices below the share price would be trading at lower values:

- Strike Price $90. This option is currently trading at $4, so total price is $4 x 100 = $400.
- Strike Price $80. This option is trading at $3, total price $300.

- Strike Price $60. This option is trading at $1, total price $100.

The numbers and strike prices here are not necessarily realistic but chosen for illustration purposes so that you can understand how options trading works.

When the option reaches zero days to expiration, the price of the option is strictly the difference between the strike price and the share price. For simplicity, suppose that the share price was $100 with zero days left to expiration. Let's write down what our in the money calls were priced at 30 days out:

- Strike Price $90. This option is currently trading at $7, so total price is $7 x 100 = $700.
- Strike Price $80. This option is trading at $10, a total price of $1,000.
- Strike Price $60. This option is trading at $20, the total price of $2,000.

Now, the prices will be the difference between the strike and share price:

- Strike Price $90. This option is currently worth $10, so total price is $10 x 100 = $1,000.
- Strike Price $80. This option is worth $20, the total price of $2,000.
- Strike Price $60. This option is worth $40, the total price of $4,000.

So at zero days, you could buy the option with the $60 share price for $4,000, but you'd have to buy the shares for $60 x 100 = $6,000. So, you're in for $10,000. Then you could sell them for $100 and break even (well actually you'd lose because of commissions) or hold onto the shares hoping they would go up. Bottom line? You want to buy options contracts before they expire. This is because the time value has run out. Time value is part of the pricing and now its $0. Time value is also called extrinsic value.

When there's more time, there's more money

The price of the options contract is affected by the distance between the strike price and the share price. It is also affected by the time left on the options contract. Time value decreases as the expiration date approaches. Or put another way, the price of an option drops as the time left on the options contract decreases. The relationship between price and time left on the contract is exponential, that is the price of the option begins dropping rapidly as the time left on the contract decreases. For example, we could have something like the following:

- Price of an option 90 days out $1,000
- Price of an option 45 days out $500
- Price of an option 30 days out $250
- Price of an option 10 days out $100

The drop-in price as time passes is called time decay. Again, the numbers are for illustration only to illustrate the point. You can watch some real options on the market to see how they actually behave (but remember the prices are also influenced by the underlying stock price). Time value is always decaying.

Volatility

This is the last factor that works into pricing when trading options. Volatility tells you how much and how often the price of the stock swings up and down. More volatility means more risk to the person who owns the shares of stock. Option prices are higher for more volatile stocks. Volatility can change with time.

Options – better than stocks?

Options trading provides a huge ROI as compared to stocks. This is part of the power of leverage. I am going to borrow a real example that was explained in a YouTube video discussing buying options for Apple stock. At the time, Apple was $515 per share. So that means 100 shares would cost $51,500. When the stock went up to $530, you could have sold, realizing a $15 gain on each share. With 100 shares, this translates into a profit of $1,500. The ROI or return on investment is:

ROI = % on yield = $1,500/$51,500 *100 = 2.9%

Most people would consider that a great return. But now look at what would happen had you invested in options instead, with a $520 strike price. At the time one three-month contract with that strike price had a premium of $1,990. So, you're able to invest at a much smaller price. When the shares beat the strike price, you get a profit of $630. A profit of $630 on a $1,990 investment is much better. Specifically:

ROI = % on yield = $630/$1,990 *100 = 31.1%

Honestly, that is pretty incredible. As you grow then you can invest in multiple options contracts, and the amount of profit as compared to direct stock market investing is quite astounding. Imagine if you had invested $51,500 in options instead of the stock...

Chapter 5: Options Trading Strategies

In this chapter, we will discuss some strategies for trading options.

Vertical Spreads

A vertical spread is the combination of a call and a put with different strike prices but the same expiration date. A vertical spread is simultaneously trading both options. This is done to minimize risk. Suppose that XYZ is trading at $90. We can sell a naked call at $3 with a strike price of $100. Everything is fine, we made $300 if the share price never goes above $100. If it happens to go to $120, however, then we are in big trouble with a huge loss.

But we can buy a call to act as insurance that can offset some losses if they happen. So, we simultaneously buy a call with a strike price that's a little higher than our naked call, say $105. This will come with a lower premium (since its strike is further away from the share price). Say it's $1.50. Total cost $150.

In the event that the share price does skyrocket to $120, then we are out of luck on our naked call. It's a loss and we calculate that as follows:

Loss – 100 shares at $3 with strike price $20 below share price = $2,000 - $300 premium = $1,700

However, we profit from the call we bought for $150. We make $15 per share x 100 shares = $1,500, minus the cost = $1,350. Our total loss will be:

$1,700 - $1,350 = 350

So, we only end up losing $350.

Now suppose that the share price stayed below $100. That means both contracts are worthless, but we keep the $300 premium from the call we sold. However, we lost $150 from the call we purchased. We still profit, however, at $300-$150 = $150.

Iron Condor

The Iron Condor gives you some insurance against time decay. With an iron condor, you simultaneously sell a call and a put. You do this hoping that the stock price will stay in between the strike prices, with the strike price of the call higher than the strike price of the put. For insurance, you buy a call and a put that have strike prices further out from the share prices than the call and put that you sold.

The options we sell are naked options. These have unlimited risk if the stock price went outside the strike price. So, for example, if XYZ was trading at $80, we could sell a call at $90 and sell a put at $60, hoping the price of the stock would stay in that range until expiration, and then we could profit from the premium. Suppose they were $2 each.

Then you buy a call at a strike of $100 for $1 and buy a put with a strike of $50 for $1. You can actually do an iron condor as one single trade, so it's not as complicated as this looks.

If the stock stays within the strike prices of the options we sold, then we pocket the premiums which at $2 gives us $200 + $200 = $400. The options we bought for $1, expired worthless. So, we are out the premiums, which were $1, so a total of $200. That leaves us with a total profit of $200.

The call and put we bought were insurance. They can also minimize losses if the stock goes above the naked call we sold.

Suppose that it goes to $110. The two puts expire worthlessly. We net $100 from the puts, with the $200 premium on the put we sold, and then we lost $100 on the "insurance" put we bought.

For the calls, the $90 call we sold for $2 is 20 points below, so we lost $2,000. Since we sold it for $200, our loss so far is $1,800. Now we'll see how the second call we bought acts as insurance. The call we bought for $1 with a strike of $100 is 10 points below, so we earn $1,000 from that one. It cost us $100 though, so we are left with $900. Our net loss from the calls is $900. Adding in the net profit from the puts, the total trade lost $800. Now we could have lost $1,600 – if the original call and put were all we had. So, the iron condor cut our losses in half.

In the event the stock price dropped, the logic would be the same, but with the role of puts and calls reversed.

Chapter 6: Top Mistakes made by New Traders

Swing trading isn't as risky as day trading, but it does still carry risks. Let's look at the top mistakes made by new swing traders.

Failing to use a stop-loss
Always use a stop loss on your orders so that you minimize potential losses.

Risking too much on a trade
Remember to only risk 1-2% of the capital in your investment account on an individual trade.

Not being careful with leverage
Remember swing traders can use 2:1 leverage. If you're careless, this can get you into big financial trouble.

Letting yourself be driven by emotion

Many new traders get worked up with emotion watching securities move. During this experience, they can get impatient or find themselves fearing they will miss out on a big win. However, this leads to bad moves by the trader, selling too soon or throwing too much money after something they think is a sure thing that turns out to be a bust. Or maybe they enter the trade too early. Instead of being driven by emotions in the heat of the moment new traders need to stay focused on using the analysis and techniques described in this book and go into deeper research to learn more.

Unrealistic Expectations

Swing trading is not a get rich quick scheme. Many new traders have unrealistic expectations that they will become a millionaire overnight. Not only does it take time to become a successful trader and build wealth, but it takes an awful lot of hard work. To become a successful trader, you have to spend a lot of time studying the markets, paying attention to financial news, learning how to read charts, studying the companies and so on. None of this is easy, it takes work.

Giving in to panic

Panic can lead traders to sell and take losses or fail to realize gains they could have had. Again, this is an emotional response. Instead of fearing that you'll lose everything you should follow the suggested rules for risk and always use stop loss orders to minimize potential losses.

Greed

Staying in a trade too long in the hopes of getting rich quick has undone many new investors. A new trader should set profit goals for each trade and stick with them. Use OCO orders so that the order takes care of the profits as well as the losses for you so that you don't stay in a position too long and then miss out on profits, losing money instead as the stock price declines.

Getting arrogant after a few wins

In the event that you rack up a few successful trades, you might get cocky about it and become overconfident. But be aware, if you are not careful the bad trades will find you and the losses will come. Getting arrogant rather than maintaining a humble attitude which will lead you to carefully study the markets and taking precautions while shooting for realistic profits can lead to big trouble over the longer term.

Failing to Plan

Trading for the hell of it is not a plan. Neither is trading hoping that millions will come, so trading as if you are playing the lottery, this is not a good strategy to follow. You need to lay out a specific plan before you place your first trade. Have realistic goals and always know what your goals are. Once you meet the goals then you can readjust. Your goals should be modest in the beginning, that way they will be easier to meet. Set out ahead of time how much capital you are going to risk and what your specific goals for profit are going to be. When you meet your goals, don't blow it by losing focus. Set more realistic and attainable goals with reasonable levels of risk.

Failing to take time to learn

Congratulations! No, I mean that seriously. By reading this book, you have already shown that you are the kind of person who is willing to sit down and take the time to learn about the markets before diving in. However, there is a lot to learn about stocks, trading, and options. You should be constantly learning, reading as many books as possible, watching YouTube videos, and taking a training course. You may also benefit from personally getting to know other traders in your area to learn from them and trade experiences. The stock market is very complicated, and even seasoned veterans make large mistakes and lose a lot of money. You can never learn enough about it so be sure to keep putting in the time to improve your knowledge. When it comes to the stock market, trading, and options, you should consider yourself a lifelong learner.

Don't buy out of the money options

Out of the money options are cheap, however, remember that the probability of the stock moving enough to turn an out of the money option to one that is in the money is relatively low. An out of the money option is a bad way to invest.

Ignoring Time Value

Remember that the three things that impact the price of an option are whether it's in the money or out of the money, that is what the strike price is relative to the current stock price, volatility, and time value. Time value always decreases with each passing day, so you need to know where the option stands with respect to time value.

Buying options close to expiration

This is somewhat similar to buying options that are out of the money. As an option gets closer to expiration, they get cheaper. New traders think they are snapping up bargains by buying options that are close to expiration. However, the closer an option gets to expiration, the more worthless it becomes especially if it's out of the money. Buying an option that is both out of the money and close to expiration would be a really bad move.

Trade in the right time frames

Swing trading is a short-term activity, but it's not day trading. How long a time frame is involved depends on whom you ask. Many swing traders will be trading on a 2-6-day time frame. If that isn't comfortable for you, that's fine. You can always stretch it out further, even out to 100 days or so. But don't be so risk averse that you fail to exit your positions. If that becomes an issue maybe long-term investing is more your style. On the other hand, if you find that swing trading isn't exciting enough when you've put together enough capital to open an account (you are going to need $25,000 at a minimum) then maybe day trading is where you belong. The reality is that you are going to have more success trading at a level that is most comfortable for you. Don't swing trade because other people think day trading is too dangerous or do it because you're a long term investor who's getting mocked by their trading friends.

Chapter 7: Special tips for Swing Traders

In this chapter, we will provide some tips, especially for swing traders. Swing trading isn't as well known or popular as day trading or simply investing so it will help to review the basic principles that you may not be hearing in general.

The trend is your friend

The biggest lesson about swing trading, although there are some swing traders who fade or short, is that the uptrend is what most swing traders are looking for. With this in mind, spend time studying all the signals that you can so that you can take advantage of opportunities early on. You should also become deeply familiar with candles and learn to recognize the signals that candles can give you about developing trends and reversals in the market.

Follow the big trends

Traders often get too focused on individual stocks. Of course, that is the ultimate name of the game but don't forget that these stocks are trading in a larger world and that sometimes the trends seen in the overall market are going to be very impactful. One place that we haven't talked about but where you should be focusing your attention is on the S & P 500. This index is a very good measure of where the overall market is heading. Of course, on a detailed level, individual stocks are not going to be following any given index, but for longer-term trends, the S & P 500 and other indexes are going to set the tone that most will be following. So, you can learn a lot about the state of the market by paying close attention to it. Larger market trends often have a nasty habit of asserting themselves on individual stocks. So, it's always a good idea to know what those larger trends are doing and to take them to be yet one more signal that you should take into consideration before making any trading moves. The S & P 500 is also going to be very sensitive to big news and events so you may be able to get wind that something is happening that has large institutional investors spooked (or happy about) by looking at the big indexes. They get news before you do, and while you may not have the news yet by tracking trends in the big indices you may be able to deduce that something is going on even if you don't know what that is in detail yet.

Don't be a one-way trader

When appropriate, you should be ready to short. With options trading, you can use puts for insurance purposes as well. If you are a bullish investor, don't get too caught up in it and become a rigid dinosaur. There are opportunities for bearish investors too, so you should be ready to take them when they arise. This also works vice versa. Some people like shorting so forget about basic investing. You shouldn't do that either.

Don't rely on short term charts all the time

Short term charts are important. After all, you're looking to buy and sell your stocks over short time periods and not hold them for years. That said, you need to keep the big picture in mind. That means studying longer-term charts for various time periods.

Never stop practicing

It is a good idea to continually hone your skills with simulators. That way you can learn to swing trade without risking real capital. This will help you become a seasoned investor without having to take all the risks that people who came before you took. People don't like to practice, but can you imagine how NBA games would go if nobody practiced? Even the best basketball players in the world devote a significant amount of time to practicing and training. Why should you, as a professional in your own area of expertise, be any different?

Don't ignore beta

Volatile stocks can carry some risk. However, you can also profit from them as well. Moves by stocks with a high beta can far surpass moves by the indexes themselves. Knowing what you know about options, use puts for insurance and get involved with more volatile stocks. Just don't put all your eggs in one basket. But volatile stocks can offer you some solid opportunities for growth.

Study Charts over different time frames

To really understand a given stock, you should know how it's been behaving on multiple time frames. Study long term (two years) weekly charts for the stock. Also, study the fine details of the stock's movement on daily charts. If you are going to risk your precious money on a stock, then you really need to know how it behaves at all levels. It's too easy for shorter-term traders to get lost in the short term only.

Enter Trends at the Beginning

Bailing at the bottom of a downturn and buying up stock at the top of an upturn are things that people who don't know anything about stock markets do. They want to sell their shares and stuff the money in their mattress. As a real trader, especially if you want to be a swing trader, you need to really study trends, reversals, supports, and resistance. The goal is to be able to get in on trends as early as possible. You should also learn to recognize when things are too late and use options for insurance policies. If you come in when it is too late to hit a peak, you can still gain from the trend by shorting. But you need to be able to recognize where you stand relative to the trend. If a stock is peaking, this is actually early for the bearish traders, but late for the bullish traders. A good trader is bearish or bullish depending on the situation. So if you missed out on an upward trend, then you can still profit on the downside. But be ready to do so when you spot what's happening.

Getting in on trends early helps minimize risk and it also helps you maximize your profits.

Use Multiple Indicators

One mistake that new swing traders make is putting too much faith in a single indicator. It sounds very sophisticated so you can be forgiven for thinking that the right candle is a sure thing, or that you can't go wrong with a golden cross. The reality is that underlying the order is chaos. The stock market is inherently unpredictable except in the long term. You can never be sure of a belief in the direction of a stock, you can only minimize probabilities of being wrong. The way that you do this is by utilizing multiple tools simultaneously. When one indicator is giving you a strong signal, don't just run with it, you need to check that signal against all the other ones that you know.

Get up early and watch financial news

The first thing you need to do each morning is, first, get up early. You really need to hit the ground to be a successful trader. Then watch the financial news and read financial websites and publications. Scan the financial news for information about stocks and options you're already holding and also looking for information about securities you plan to trade later. You are not going to get the information as fast, detailed, and furious as the large institutional investors are going to, but you still need to stay on top of what's happening.

Avoid Impulse Buying

While swing trading isn't day trading, it can instill some bad habits. One possible bad habit you might pick up is getting into impulse buying. Now and then, impulse buying will turn out to be profitable. However, it's not always going to work out. Impulse buying is really nothing more than gambling. A swing trader is not a gambler.

Capital Preservation is a Value

If you run out of capital, your trading days are over. It also shows that you are a reckless trader. If you find yourself unable to preserve the capital in your account, then maybe you should just invest in mutual funds. You're letting your emotions get a hold of you if you find out that you are running out of money. The thing to do is step back and breath if you find yourself in the midst of a string of losses. Don't panic and try to make rash moves in desperate attempts to get your money back. You might even want to stop and step back from the markets for a few days to keep a bad situation from spinning out of control. Beforehand, always set a stop-loss when you make a trade. This will help keep losses to a minimum, which should be a maximum risk of about 7% for your entire account. You should also use limit orders judiciously.

Don't trip over dollars to pick up pennies

While we spend a lot of time talking about minimizing risk, some traders are far too conservative. There is no sense in getting into trading to make a few cents off dollar trades. If you take a hyper-conservative approach to trading, then you will never see yourself getting anywhere. The tools exist that will help you take reasonable risks. Make sure you pick entry points that have more upside than risk. This is like any other business, if you are not making profits there is no point in trading. Some restaurants shut down on certain days or only serve lunch while their competitors are raking in all the money. So not taking unwarranted risks is certainly reasonable but getting into trades to make ten cents is not reasonable.

Never pull a stop order

Hope and desperation can get the best of anybody, especially when money is involved. A big mistake many new swing trader make is to pull a stop order, even though their trade is on a downturn. This can stem from hope, a desperate hope that it's going to turn back around, because well, it was a sure thing! However, if your trade is dropping close to stop order territory, that is probably a signal you shouldn't ignore. It is the market telling you that it's going to go down further from that and there isn't going to be any recovery this time. You don't know how big a loss is going to be and ignoring the signals because you hope something will turn back into an upswing is a bad gambling strategy, not trading. Remember every big loss got started somewhere, and at one time the $20,000 loss was only $500. Stop orders are there for a reason and a disciplined trader doesn't operate without them.

Chapter 8: The Mindset of the Swing Trader

Being a swing trader is a different kind of occupation. Most people are too risk-averse to try and enter this world, so it takes a special kind of mindset. A swing trader needs to have a higher level of mental toughness, but also needs to be extremely rational to the point of scientific precision.

Keep a good mental attitude

When swing trading, you may be doing it from home, in fact, you probably will. This can make it difficult to keep a good mental attitude. The reason is you may be in for some major setbacks. This can happen even when you've gained a lot of experience, but it's certainly going to happen when you're a beginner. If you have multiple setbacks in a row it can be hard to keep your chin up. Don't let negative emotions take over. Should bad trades just be blown off? Absolutely not. But you don't want to dwell on them either.

Dwelling on a bad trade is counterproductive. That isn't to say that you shouldn't learn from your bad trades. The point is to learn the lessons you need to learn and move on as fast as possible.

Maintain detailed records

Make sure you know what you did and when you did it. This is part of learning when mistakes were made. Note down what signals you are looking at to get into or exit a position. That way when it didn't work out you can go back and look at the charts and compare to your notes to see where you went wrong. We all need to learn from our mistakes, and by detailing things it will help you learn quickly and avoid making the same mistake again and again.

Be ready to move ahead

Some people get emotionally wiped out from a bad trade. That isn't going to help you establish a career as a swing trader. If you make a bad trade, learn from your mistake and then get right back in the saddle. You need to move forward into making your next trade, not impulsively, but as soon as you've learned from your mistakes.

Making a bad trade can seem like a personal failure. Many beginning swing traders get lost in the old game of "why didn't I do this" and "could have, would have, should have". Again, use your mind and not your emotions in swing trading. That means when you have a bad trade, you aren't going to take it as a personal failure and beat yourself up about it. Instead, you are going to apply the tools of reason and learn from the mistakes.

You also have to realize that you're not going to be able to capitalize on every little opportunity that comes up. We can all pull up stock charts right now and see when some stock had a huge move to the upside. If only we had bought shares! You have to remember that you're not going to get in on every possible win. And you also have to remember that there is always tomorrow. The markets aren't going anywhere, so if you were at lunch with the cousins passing through town when a stock you were interested in took a big ride up, and you missed out, don't sweat it. Just come back tomorrow looking for new opportunities. They are always coming.

Conclusion

I'd like to thank you for reading How to Trade Options: Swing Trading. I hope that you found this book informative and educational. I would also like to think that I helped broaden out your mind a little bit. Many people haven't heard about swing trading and don't realize the options it can provide. Also, we hope that you found our chapters on options useful so that you can combine what you've learned about swing trading and what you now know about the underlying dynamics of the stock market with options and options trading.

Swing trading offers more ambitious investors the opportunity to play an active role in the markets that is a bit safer and less dramatic as day trading but is certainly as interesting. Moreover, it uses many of the same tools but you're at far less risk of completely blowing it. Some people may use swing trading as an intermediate step, after wetting your toes with it you may decide that you want to take things up another level and get involved with day trading. And that is perfectly fine if you do. For those who aren't inclined to day trading, swing trading can be extremely lucrative with more upside and fewer risks. So, you've come to the right place.

Options also offer lots of golden opportunities. They let you get into trades without risking much capital and can provide much higher ROI than stock trading. You can grow with options trading and soon you might be investing as much as you would have with stocks but find yourself earning far higher profits. They are also fun and exciting.

Remember that no matter what path you take, continuing education is vital for the trader. We have barely scratched the surface with this small book. There are many resources available online including paid courses, free articles, free videos, and more. Plus, there are lots and lots of books to read on these topics.

Keep up the work of taking in new knowledge so that you can continue to improve your trading skills.

I would like to thank you again for taking the precious time to read this small book and I hope it helps you reach your trading goals. Be sure to drop on Amazon and leave a review – we will certainly appreciate it!

Made in the USA
Monee, IL
23 February 2020